# Walking
# with Welsh Legends
## Central Wales

Graham Watkins

First published in 2013

© Graham Watkins

© Llygad Gwalch 2013

ISBN: 978-1-84524-191-9

Cover design: Lynwen Jones

Published by Llygad Gwalch,
12 Iard yr Orsaf, Llanrwst, Wales LL26 0EH.
tel: 01492 624031
fax: 01492 641502
email: books@carreg-gwalch.com
internet: www.carreg-gwalch.com

*This book is dedicated
to the people from all walks of life
who look after the beautiful countryside of Wales,
and protect its heritage for us all to enjoy.*

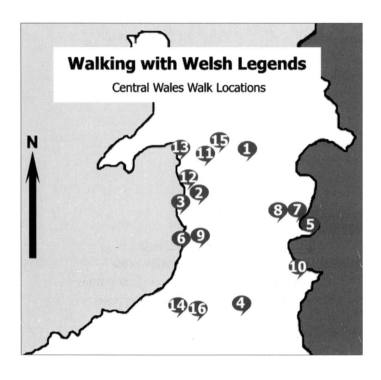

# Walking with Welsh Legends

Central Wales Walk Locations

# Contents

# Introduction

In this book, the third in the series *Walking with Welsh Legends*, you will find sixteen stories, each relating to a particular place in central Wales. Alongside each story is a walk, giving you the opportunity to explore beautiful countryside and understand the geography of each narrative. Rugged mountains, castles, golden beaches, hidden valleys, lakes and stunning waterfalls all provide a spectacular backdrop, helping to bring each legend to life.

Owain Glyndŵr, the Red Dragon of Wales, the Five Saints and the Red Bandits of Mawddwy are just a few of the characters you will meet in these pages. Learn where the Red Dragon of Wales lives today; how the drovers travelled the land and created their own banking system; and how King Arthur destroyed the evil monster they called the Barfog. Discover the Lost Land of Wales, the Salt Smugglers of Mawddach and the secret of the Robber's Grave.

Many pieces of Welsh folklore are repeated and there are variations of the same story relating to different places. At the same time, some places are associated with several legends. To avoid confusion and repetition, where legends are similar, I have used the story I liked best and omitted the rest.

The legends I have included are a diverse mixture. There are love stories, tales of heroic deeds, foolishness, greed, fables and humour. The cast includes fair maidens, wicked tyrants, explorers, a headless dog, kings, and ordinary folk quietly going about their business.

The walks are equally diverse and include mountains, sandy beaches, castles, woodland, hidden lakes and ancient towns. As I completed each walk, I found that I had a different perspective on, and a better insight into, the related legend. The walk and legend reinforced each other and added to the enjoyment. Most of the walks are not difficult and suitable for a family to attempt together. To receive the most enjoyment, I suggest that you read the legend first and look at the map to help understand the geography of the story, before you start the walk. By doing so you will be able to pick out the relevant landmarks as you go.

The starting point for each walk can be located using the latitude and longitude coordinates given, or the map references quoted from Ordnance Survey 1:50,000 Landranger Maps. I make no claims regarding rights of way but have walked all of the routes without any problems. Equipment I would recommend includes a compass, an Ordnance Survey map, suitable footwear and appropriate clothing. The weather can change quickly, particularly on higher ground, so dress accordingly and, if it is hot, sun-cream, hats and drinking water for everyone are essential.

For those who may be interested, I have Anquet software to plot the waypoints on a computer and download them to a Garmin Etrex Venture HC to do each walk. My wife bought the GPS for my birthday after we got lost on one of the walks. As a consequence, these are toys that I have learned to use whilst researching Welsh legends and walks. They have added another dimension to the planning and I would not go walking without them now. Apart from the fact that it is a lot harder to get lost, I find the information they give me both invaluable and entertaining. One Anquet function I particularly like allows you to fly over the route, viewing it using pictures from Google earth. Great fun! Many of the walks are well-signposted, but some of the more remote ones are not and it is easy to get lost.

A word about walking speed is appropriate. I read somewhere that the British Army used to march 3 miles (4.83 km) in 50 minutes and then rest for 10 minutes before marching the next 3 miles. The speed I have quoted is rather slower at 2 miles (3.2 km) per hour with an hour added for each 300 metres of climb. This is the same speed that the Welsh Drovers used to walk, when driving stock across the country. It will seem slow for some – but what is the point of a pleasant walk if you don't have time to admire the views or smell the flowers on the way?

I should also take this opportunity to thank my wife for her good humour and sense of direction when lost, and thank Dave Simkins FCCA, Graham Watkins (my cousin), Rosemary Riches and Cheryl Matthews for their constructive comments, which helped immensely. While the position of features is right at the time of writing this guide, the location of stiles and gates may change from time to time and new fences and stiles sometimes get added, confusing the unwary. Many of the walks include working farmland, and I would urge everyone to observe the normal courtesies of closing gates behind you if they are shut when you reach them, taking home your litter and keeping dogs under control. If you do, we will all enjoy the beauty and splendour of Wales and her legends.

*Graham Watkins*
*Garnlwyd 2013*

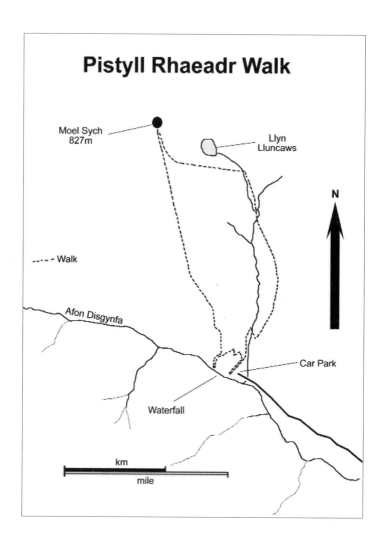

# Pistyll Rhaeadr Walk

Moel Sych
827m

Llyn
Lluncaws

N

- - - Walk

Afon Disgynfa

Car Park

Waterfall

km

mile

# 1

# The Land of the Dead

Gwyn ap Nudd was King of the Underworld, and the mountains of Cadair Berwyn and Moel Sych his throne. His was a cold, barren kingdom, filled with foul swamps, evil vipers and devils. This was the land of the dead, a dangerous desolate place seldom visited by mortals. The gateway to this distant kingdom was Pistyll Rhaeadr, and each night Gwyn ap Nudd would leave his kingdom to stalk the lands of Wales, collecting the souls of the dead.

Mortal men who were brave or foolish enough to venture into mountains of Berwyn would find the king feasting in a fine palace. The lamps would be lit. Gold and silver plate would sparkle in the shimmering light. None could resist the king's offer to join in the feast and enjoy the sumptuous food and wine that was being offered. As they ate the meats and fruits and drank the fine wines, Gwyn ap Nudd would steal their souls and throw them onto the mountain where they would lay tormented until time ended. None ever returned to their homes or their loved ones.

Wives cried for their husband and children mourned their lost fathers. Wary of calling out loud lest they upset Gwyn ap Nudd, people whispered about the missing souls. Slowly the stories of how no one ever returned from the mountain above Pistyll Rhaeadr spread across the land.

In Llangollen, St Collen listened intently as the tales of woe were repeated in hushed tones. Seeing that this was the devil's work, he at once determined to climb the mountain and put an end to the misery.

Armed only with a small bottle of holy water, the saint set out on his perilous quest. As he walked he wondered what had happened to the missing people. He arrived at the little village of Llanrhaeadr ym Mochnant to find the people fearful. A dark cloud hung over the once beautiful valley and pressed up against the mountain filling the air with damp, putrid air.

St Collen walked on up the valley, following the river until he came to a great waterfall. The icy water poured down from the mountain with a defiant roar that chilled his blood. Slowly the saint picked his way across the rocks and began to climb. As he climbed the air grew colder and the damp soaked through his cloak, mixing with his hot sweat. He reached the top of the waterfall, where a cold wind sliced through his wet clothing and chilled him to the bone. Exhausted by the climb, he sat and rested. The sky grew dark and rain began to fall. St Collen began to shake violently, his frozen body aching with cold. He could feel evil in the air.

Standing up, St Collen started to walk north towards the higher mountains. Beneath his feet the ground was fetid with decay and his legs sank into the mud. Slowly he made his way forward, climbing as he went. After many hours trudging through the slime, until unable to go further, he sank down on his knees and wept. He knew he could not go on. As he knelt, the wind gusted and a voice howled across the mountain, 'Why do you weep? Come. Here is warmth and food and wine that will warm your very innards.'

St Collen peered into the mist and saw a bright light twinkling in the distance. He pulled himself to his feet and stumbled on. Getting closer, he saw a fine palace blazing with radiant illumination. The doors were open and a stream of light poured out. He could smell tempting food being cooked. He went into the palace. Inside, sat on a great throne, was a giant of a man. In one hand he held a huge golden goblet and in the other a leg of beef. Below him was a table laid to overflowing with gold and silver plates laden with fine foods of every description.

'Who are you?' demanded St Collen.

'Who am I, you ask. I am Gwyn ap Nudd, King of the Underworld, and this is my house. Come and join me. We will eat and drink together,' said the king.

St Collen crossed the floor and sat on a stool near the king. He looked at the table piled high with food.

'You must be hungry after your climb. Help yourself,' snorted the king as he chewed on his beef.

But although he was hungry, St Collen did not eat, and although he was thirsty, he did not drink. Instead he opened his cloak and drew out the small bottle of holy water that he had bought with him and drank sparingly. Then he replaced the bottle in his pocket and sat quietly looking at the king. Gwyn ap Nudd continued to feast, pretending to ignore his visitor but watching the saint slyly as he did so, and wondering why the mortal did not eat or drink. This had never happened before.

After some hours the king grew tired of eating and drinking. He wiped his mouth on his sleeve and sat back in his throne eyeing the saint with suspicion.

'Why have you come to my table and insulted me by refusing my hospitality?' he yelled. 'Come, humour me by tasting a little of this fine fruit,' he said more quietly, pointing to the table.

'Why do you steal the souls of the living?' asked the saint.

'The souls of all mortals belong to me!' answered the king.

'Not before their time,' replied Collen.

Gwyn ap Nudd and Collen debated and argued for days over who owned the souls of the living. The heated discussion went back and forth as the king ate and drank heartily, eagerly encouraging his opponent to join him. Collen saw this was a trap. He did not eat a morsel of food or touch a drop of wine. Instead he took tiny sips of holy water to keep refreshed.

The king grew tired of the argument. He saw that he would never win against the quiet saint. As he argued he knew his grip over mortal men was slipping away. Slowly, as the King of the Underworld ran out of arguments, his palace began to fade. Before long it had vanished forever, taking Gwyn ap Nudd with it.

Collen found himself sitting on a pile of stones on the top of the mountain. All that was left of the palace below him was a deep hollow where the king's throne had been. The sun was shining on Moel Sych and the birds were singing as Collen trudged wearily down the mountain. His work was done.

*Looking north. Moel Sych is in the far distance on the left. The clouds and mist make it a dark and brooding place.*

# Pistyll Rhaeadr Walk

The Berwyn mountains are remote and majestic. Less well-known than Snowdonia (*Eryri*) or the Brecon Beacons (*Bannau Brycheiniog*), the Berwyns are, nonetheless, well worth exploring. This walk begins at Pistyll Rhaeadr waterfall, where Afon Disgynfa drops 240 feet. The waterfall is taller than Niagara Falls – the tallest waterfall in Wales and England – and in the eighteenth century was named by a poet as one of the seven wonders of Wales.

From the base of the waterfall the walk travels along an ancient drovers' route up through Cwm Nant-y-Llyn valley to Llyn Lluncaws. Here it continues ascending to the top of Moel Sych before returning, along the mountain ridge, to the waterfall. Pistyll Rhaeadr is 10½ miles south-west of Llangollen and 14 miles west of Oswestry (*Croesoswallt*). To reach the waterfall, take the B4580 from Oswestry and drive to the remote village of Llanrhaeadr-ym-Mochnant. Once you are in the village a small single track road takes you a further 4 miles to the waterfall, where you will find a pay and display car park, toilets and a café (open every day of the year, reduced hours in the winter, and also does B&B).

*Ordnance Survey map number 125 grid reference SJ 072 294*
Latitude = 52.8550, Longitude = -3.3768
Lat = 52 degrees, 51.3 minutes North
Long = 3 degrees, 22.6 minutes West

| | |
|---|---|
| Length | 6.29 km – 3.91 miles |
| Maximum height | 752.09 metres |
| Minimum height | 322.54 metres |
| Height ascended | 486.29 metres |
| Navigation | Easy |
| Difficulty | Moderate |
| Estimated time | 3 hours 46 minutes |

Leave the car park and take the footpath on the left, just outside the car park entrance, so that you are walking northeast. Ignore the first gate on your left and continue uphill, turning left between stone walls, and then turn right following the footpath sign. After a short distance there is a footpath leading off to the left. Ignore this path and continue straight on along the left hand side of the valley. Leave the path where it turns sharp left and cross the Nant-y-Llyn stream using the wooden bridge.

From the bridge walk south-east for 100 metres until you reach a junction where you turn left and walk north-east up the western side of the valley with the stream on your left. The grass track you are now on is the old drovers' track over the mountain to Bala. As you ascend you pass over two stiles and the path gradually turns so that you are walking north. Below you in the valley is a group of low stone walls. These are pens used for gathering sheep that have been driven down from the mountain.

After 1.3 km the path deteriorates and is boggy as it crosses a stream and continues north for a further 500 metres to a second stream, which you also cross. The path now turns west and continues to climb bringing Llyn Lluncaws into view on your right. As you climb, the path turns to the right heading towards the summit of Moel Sych. There is an ancient cairn on the top of the mountain that marks the junction of the county boundaries of Powys, Clwyd and Gwynedd. At 827 metres, Moel Sych is the twenty-ninth highest mountain in Wales and there are good views in all directions.

Leaving the cairn, walk south following the fence, keeping it on your right. After descending for 800 metres the path climbs, taking you over a smooth peak before descending once again. The exact location of the path becomes unclear, but to avoid boggy areas you may prefer to climb over the fence and walk with the fence on your left. (There was a stile here, which for some reason has been dismantled.)

Follow the line of fencing downhill until it ends. The footpath continues, turning slightly to the east, and becomes a grassy path as the ground improves. Aim for the cliffs in the distance as you descend. As the path gets steeper it begins to zig-zag, eventually bringing you to an intersection with a track. Go straight across the track and walk towards a kissing gate located in a stone wall. Continue through the gate and walk

*The waterfall, Pistyll Rhaeadr*

200 metres to the head of the waterfall. Below you sits the Tanat valley. It is believed that wine was produced here in Roman times. Although the Romans and their vines have long since disappeared from Wales, Tanat wine is still produced in Italy.

Leave the head of the waterfall through the same kissing gate and walk up the track, where you turn right so that you are walking north-east. After a short distance the track begins to descend and you reach a yellow arrow pointing to some steps on the right. Follow the steps downhill until they rejoin the track, taking you back to the car park at the bottom of the waterfall.

19

# Machynlleth Walk

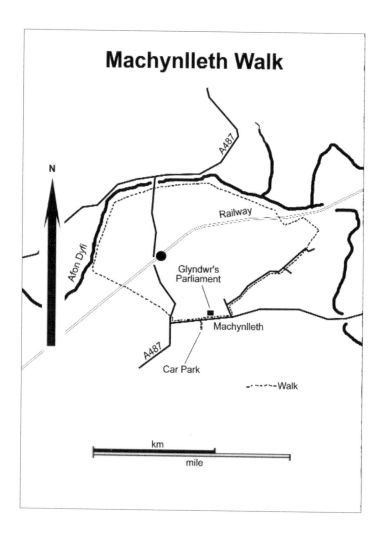

N

A487

Railway

Afon Dyfi

Glyndwr's
Parliament

A487

Machynlleth

Car Park

- - - - - Walk

km

mile

## 2

# Owain Glyndŵr

The start of the fifteenth century saw an uprising against the English occupiers of Wales that resulted in the first independent Welsh parliament. The leader of the rebellion, Owain Glyndŵr, was descended from the Princes of Powys and Cyfeiliog in the north and, on his mother's side, the kingdom of Deheubarth in the south. His royal lineage gave him a strong claim to the Welsh throne.

Glyndŵr was given a training in law in London, and trained as a soldier, serving with distinction for the English king in 1384 and 1387 before returning to Wales. Henry IV had come to the English throne, and there was no job for Glyndŵr in Henry's army.

The Wales Owain came back to was in turmoil. The murder of Llywelyn ein Llyw Olaf at Cilmeri, and the harsh treatment of the Welsh by Edward I, had left the people smouldering with resentment. Colonial towns, defended by strong castles, had economical and racial privileges, while the native Welsh population were no more than serfs in their own land.

The Welsh people were cowed and there was no justice in the law. They wanted a leader – and charismatic Glyndŵr was the man of the hour. He found himself drawn into a quarrel with Reginald de Grey, Lord of Ruthin, who had stolen some land. De Grey was close to the king, and his private argument with Glyndŵr quickly developed into feudal warfare.

Glyndŵr gathered loyal supporters around him and

established an army at Ruthin. He raised his battle flag on 16 September 1400 and started to drive out the English. Glyndŵr was fifty-one years old. Ruthin fell, and Glyndŵr followed up with attacks throughout northern Wales. His followers declared him the rightful prince of Wales, and Welshmen threw down their tools and hurried back to Wales to join him. Welsh archers deserted the English to join Glyndŵr. University students abandoned their studies at Oxford and returned to Wales eager to fight. Glyndŵr's stated mission was to reject Henry IV as the king of Wales, and to eject the English from his country.

The English response was brutal. They levied a large army and attempted to put Glyndŵr's rebellion down by invading and destroying the country. No trace was found of Glyndŵr and his followers, and eventually the English government resorted to penal statutes designed to punish Wales. The effect of this was to drive more Welshmen to take up arms.

Glyndŵr and his men hid in the mountains for the winter, emerging the following year with a renewed campaign. They seized castles, including Harlech, Conwy and Aberystwyth. By 1403 the rebels operated freely throughout Wales and had won strategic battles. In 1404 Glyndŵr claimed the title of ruler of Wales. A parliament was established at Machynlleth. Treaties were made with France and Spain, whose ambassadors attended the court. Glyndŵr made a triple alliance with Edmund Mortimer, the Earl of March and Thomas Percy, the Earl of Northumberland. Plans were made to invade England and divide the country between them. French troops arrived to help the revolution and Scottish privateers raided English towns along the coast of Wales. French ships landed Welsh troops in Devon and attacked Dartmouth. Glyndŵr petitioned Pope Benedict XIII for support.

The English quickly reacted. The English army was the largest, and most effective in Europe, as the French discovered two years later at Agincourt. Castles were lost and retaken many times, but slowly the strength of the English forces wore down the Welsh. Eight years after he had raised his standard, Glyndŵr suffered a major defeat when the castles at Aberystwyth and Harlech were lost in 1408 and 1409. There was personal tragedy for Glyndŵr when Henry's forces captured his family at Harlech. His wife, Margaret, two daughters and three granddaughters were imprisoned in the Tower of London. They were all dead within seven years.

The English changed their strategy by blockading Wales. They cut off trade routes and arms supplies to squeeze the rebels, and many Welshmen started to ask for terms of surrender. The revolt struggled on, but the crushing superiority of the English was taking a dreadful toll until only a few rebels remained, conducting a guerrilla campaign. Glyndŵr became an outlaw.

The English army seized prominent landowners and executed them, attempting to discover where Glyndŵr was hiding. After more than twelve years of warfare the revolt finally petered out when pardons were offered to the last rebels. The Welsh had had enough.

Henry V replaced his father as King in 1413 and softened the English position on Wales, helping the last of the rebellion to peter out.

In 1485 English laws and customs were imposed across Wales when Henry VII was crowned King of England. He was a Welshman.

Glyndŵr never surrendered to the English and was never pardoned. Instead, he quietly disappeared into obscurity, protected by the silence of the Welsh people. One of Glyndŵr's daughters, Alys, had married, and lived in Kentchurch in Herefordshire, and there have been claims that he spent the rest of his life living with her family there, passing himself off as an elderly Franciscan Friar employed as the family tutor. The family kept his secret for nearly 600 years.

Today, Owain Glyndŵr remains a potent symbol of Welsh independence and patriotism. In his letter from Pennal to the king of France, he outlined his vision of a new Wales – with an independent church; where the Welsh language was the language of law and government; with two universities; and with its own parliament. In 1997, Wales returned a vote for self-government in a referendum, with further powers and an 'official' status added to the language in 2011. Glyndŵr's dream had become a reality.

*Bridge over the Dyfi, Machynlleth*

*Owain Glyndŵr's parliament building*

# Machynlleth Walk

This is one of the easier walks of the series, starting in the town and taking you on a circular stroll along the bank of the Dyfi as it meanders towards the sea. Machynlleth is located 18 miles north east of Aberystwyth along the A487 and 10 miles east of Aberdyfi on the A493. There is a pay and display car park with nearby toilets located in the centre of the town on Heol Maengwyn.

*Ordnance Survey map number 135 grid reference SH 748 007*
Latitude = 52.5899, Longitude = -3.8503
Lat = 52 degrees, 35.4 minutes North
Long = 3 degrees, 51.0 minutes West

| | |
|---|---|
| Length | 4.89 km – 3.03 miles. |
| Maximum height | 36.61 metres |
| Minimum height | 5.25 metres |
| Height ascended | 58.94 metres |
| Navigation | Easy |
| Difficulty | Easy |
| Estimated time | 1 hours 42 minutes |

Leave the car park via the main entrance and turn right along Heol Maengwyn. On your left you will pass an old stone building with a slate roof and a grey plaque on the wall. This is reputed to be the building where Owain Glyndŵr held his first parliament in 1404. There is a second smaller plaque commemorating a visit made by Queen Elizabeth II in July 1986.

Continue along the main street until you reach Garth Road, a turning to the left, which you take so that the community hospital is on your right. After a short distance you turn right and walk north-east, keeping the hospital on your right. Keep straight on until the road bends to the right and you reach a road with a dead end sign ahead. This is also signposted Garth Road and is the route you need to follow.

The road climbs and continues north-east for 300 metres, where it turns sharp right, and there is a signpost to Garth Holiday Park. Do not turn right here. Instead continue straight on along the stone track following the footpath sign. Follow the track for 150 metres until you arrive at a stile on your left. Cross the stile, and where the path forks immediately after the stile take the right trail. The footpath now goes across sparse woodland in a north-westerly direction for 160 metres until you reach a rocky outcrop with a single track railway with the Dyfi in the valley below you. Look east along the railway line and, depending on the weather, you will see banks of wind turbines on the distant mountains. This is the windfarm at Mynydd Cemais, one of the first to be built in Britain. When the wind blows it produces enough electricity to power 6000 homes.

The footpath now turns west and you follow it downhill to the railway line, which you cross using the two stiles and taking care to watch out for trains. Once you have crossed the railway line the path joins the riverbank and continues west. The river is not tidal at this point but does sometimes flood. The water runs fast and clear and is famous for its salmon and sea trout. Follow its course for the next 600 m to another stile leading to the next field. This brings you to a strange-looking footbridge sculpted with metal waves and fish: this bridge was made by a local man.

When you reach the footbridge, continue west keeping the river on your right. The footpath now becomes a tarmac path and leads you to a metal gate into the next field. Follow the tarmac path through two more metal gates until you arrive at an ancient five-arch stone road bridge that crosses the river. Machynlleth road bridge was built in 1533, repaired in 1681 and rebuilt in 1805 at a cost of £250. It is the gateway to northern Wales, and during the civil war a major battle was fought here for its control.

Go through the metal gates, cross the road and continue west over the stile, keeping the river on your right. After 300 metres you will reach the next stile, and the footpath follows the river as it turns south. Continue another 200 metres and cross the next stile to the next field, where you continue walking south. 350 metres further on you will reach a ladder stile leading east. This is a permissive part of the walk across a farmer's field. Once you cross the stile the path travels east across a field and then a wide grass track leads you back towards the town.

At the end of the track you reach a wide metal gate leading to a stone track. Go straight across the track and through a smaller wooden gate leading into a small field. Walk south-east across the field until you reach the railway line protected by two stiles. Go across the track and the next field, aiming for the large church ahead of you. This will lead you to two kissing gates. After the second kissing gate, walk towards the clock tower that you can see above the building and towards a small metal gate on the far right hand corner of the field.

The metal gate will bring you out at Brickfield Street where you turn right, then immediately left into Poplar Road. At the end of Poplar Road turn right along Heol Pentrerhedyn until you reach the clock tower.

The clock tower was built in the 1870s to celebrate the coming of age of Charles Stewart Vane-Tempest, Viscount Castlereagh of Plas Machynlleth, a member of the Londonderry family. The tower is considered to be unique, although there is a similar one in Leicester. In 1882 a Mr. Rees, the local watch repairer, was paid five shillings for winding the clock and maintaining it.

At the clock tower you turn left along Heol Maengwyn and follow it back to the car park.

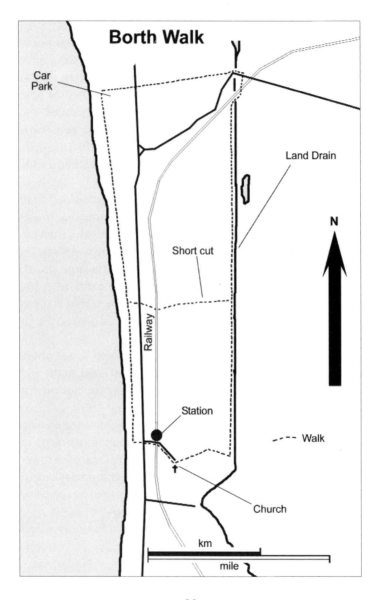

# Borth Walk

Car Park

Land Drain

N

Short cut

Railway

Station

Walk

Church

km

mile

# 3

# The Lost Land of Wales

King Gwyddno Garanhir ruled a wealthy kingdom called Cantre'r Gwaelod ( the 'bottom hundred') in an area we know today as Bae Ceredigion (*Cardigan Bay*). The kingdom was so rich and fertile that the grain stores were always full and the people of the kingdom content. The king's palace was on a hill, surrounded by villages and farms. He spent his days hunting in the great forest while his people tilled the land.

A great sea defence with two giant gates protected this fine land, which was below sea level. The guardian of the dam was a prince named Seithenyn, and it was his responsibility to open and close the sluices. Seithenyn was a seventh son and proud of the great responsibility given to him. As the youngest son, he had no wealth but the job gave him status and the people respected him.

Within the gates were giant sluices and each day, when the tide was low, Seithenyn would turn the huge wheels that opened the sluices to let the water from the 'bottom hundred' escape into the sea. Before the sea returned, he would close the sluices, keeping the tide out and the land safe.

As the years passed, Seithenyn grew bored with his job. He began to neglect the dam. Seithenyn no longer walked the dam each morning, checking for cracks. He stopped spending the afternoons putting grease on the gears that opened the sluice or painting pitch on the gates to protect them from the salt. Instead of doing his duty Seithenyn would pass each morning drinking wine as he waited for the tide to turn. Each day, after his midday meal, Seithenyn would sleep for a while and then he would drink more wine. He did not see the hinges on the gates growing rusty or notice the gears that turned the sluices slowly stiffen with age.

The marriage of Mererid, Gwyddno's daughter, was announced, and Gwyddno decreed that there would be feasting in honour of the happy couple. Musicians collected from across the land. Fine wines and beers were brewed for the occasion. Beasts were slaughtered and roasted. Huge fish were prepared for the banquet and sweet dishes by the hundred set out, ready for the feast. Everyone in the kingdom was invited to the palace.

Seithenyn dressed in his finest clothes, mounted his horse and rode to the palace. King Gwyddno greeted Seithenyn.

'This is Seithenyn, the guardian of the dam,' said the king to his noble visitors.

'Tell us, Seithenyn. Are the gates closed?' asked the king.

'They are not, sire, but the tide is out so the sluices are open,' replied Seithenyn.

'When will you shut them?' asked one of the visitors.

'I shall shut the sluices at midnight before the tide turns,' said Seithenyn.

'Leave early, Seithenyn. It's a long ride to the dam from the palace,' said the king, and turned to greet other guests.

The feast started and musicians played loudly as the people ate. The wine flowed and the feast was devoured. The clock in the tower struck nine.

'Seithenyn, the gates – you should go,' said a reveller.

'Nonsense. It's still early,' answered Seithenyn and reached for another flagon of wine.

The king and his guests danced and laughed, as the party grew louder.

The clock on the tower struck ten.

'Seithenyn, the gates – there isn't much time,' yelled King Gwyddno above the noise.

'I told you, do not worry. My horse can fly like the wind. There is plenty of time,' replied Seithenyn and drank greedily. Seithenyn's cheeks were red with wine, his laughter loud and raucous.

The clock struck eleven.

'That's enough. You are going now. That is a royal command,' snapped the king.

Seithenyn got to his feet and staggered from the palace. He mounted his horse and rode away.

The wind had started to blow from the west and the rain lashed his face. It was a fearful night. Thunder crashed between the clouds and lightning flashed across the sky. The torrent quickly turned the track to mire and the horse slowed, sinking into the slimy mud.

Suddenly, the horse missed its footing and slid into a ditch. Seithenyn landed in the mud. Groggily he stood up and began to run towards the dam.

He knew that he had to get to the gates before the tide turned. His feet slid on the mud. Brambles tore at his mud-covered clothes. Sober now, he forced himself forwards.

The sky cleared for a moment and the moon broke through. There, in front of Seithenyn, were the gates. As he staggered forward the sea, whipped up by the wind, broke through the sluices. A great wave came in from the west. The force of the rushing water breached the rotten gates and smashed the rusty hinges. The sea flooded in. The water carried Seithenyn away and he was never seen again.

King Gwyddno and a few of the revellers managed to escape and lived the rest of their lives in poverty, but the land of Cantre'r Gwaelod vanished beneath the waves. The 'bottom hundred' was lost forever, never to be seen again.

Listen carefully. Sometimes you can still hear the bells from an ancient clock tower ringing mournfully from the bottom of the sea . . .

*Borth has miles of golden sandy beaches*

# Borth Walk

This is one of the easiest walks in this series. Borth (*Y Borth*) is located on the coast 5 miles north of Aberystwyth on the B4353. The walk described is just over 8½ kilometres but can be shortened to six. Either walk is across flat easy ground including the promenade, beach and along the bank of Afon Leri. The Leri is a tidal river and part of the drainage system for the marshes beyond that are protected by levees that flank the river. The beaches at Borth are popular with holidaymakers enjoying the sand, and kite-surfers exploiting the prevailing inshore winds. The walk starts at the car park 1½ miles north of the town between the beach and the golf course. To reach the car park you need to drive across the fairway. It is also possible to park for free along the promenade where there are public toilets.

*Ordnance Survey map number 135 grid reference SN 605 924*
Latitude = 52.5127, Longitude = -4.0559
Lat = 52 degrees, 30.8 minutes North
Long = 4 degrees, 3.4 minutes West

| | |
|---|---|
| Length | 8.64 km – 5.37 miles |
| | (or 6.07 km – 3.77 miles) |
| Maximum height | 6.74 metres |
| Minimum height | 0.00 metres |
| Height ascended | 21.56 metres |
| Navigation | Easy |
| Difficulty | Easy |
| Estimated time | 2 hours 45 minutes |

Leave the car park by crossing the sea defences onto the beach and turn right so that you are walking north. Follow the beach north for 500 metres until you reach a red brick pillbox on the sand dunes. Turn right just in front of the pillbox and cross the sand dunes, following the path that takes you east across the golf course. Borth and Ynys-las Golf Club was established in 1885 and claims to be the oldest golf club in Wales. The pillbox was part of the defences for a radar station located here during the Second World War, when the threat of an invasion by the Germans from Ireland was considered likely. During the war the site was also used for testing rockets and other secret weapons. As a result, a number of derelict army buildings have been left in the area.

When you reach the road, go straight across and continue along a track between the bungalows. This will bring you to a metal gate leading to a field. Go through the gate and continue straight for 600 metres across three fields, separated by metal gates, until you reach a tarmac driveway. Go straight on along the driveway for another 250 metres, where the drive emerges onto a road and the Ynyslas Boatyard is on your left. Join the road and walk straight on across the bridge over the river until you reach the railway crossing. This is a single-track railway linking Aberystwyth and Shrewsbury, travelling along the Dyfi estuary. Cross the railway line and leave the road through a metal kissing gate on the right.

From the gate the footpath takes you south-west for 150 metres to a footbridge that crosses the river alongside the railway line. The path now turns south away from the railway line through a gate and follows the Leri, which is now on your left. The levee you are walking on is designed to trap the rising water at high tide and avoid flooding the marshland on each side of the river.

As the path progresses south you will pass a sluice gate in the far bank designed to drain the marsh at low tide. Behind you are Aberdyfi and the mountains of Snowdonia. This area is the 'Dyfi Aberleri National Nature Reserve' protecting a large variety of birds including snipe, redshank, lapwing, teal and reed bunting. You are also likely to see hen harriers and other birds of prey, as

*A tidal drainage sluice on the Leri*

well as herons fishing or sunning themselves in the mud. Walk south for 1.6 km along the river bank until you reach a junction in the path. If you turn right at the junction the path will take you west back to the beach. This is the shorter route for the walk. To complete the shorter walk you turn right at the beach and follow it north back to the car park.

To continue with the longer walk, continue straight on along the riverbank passing through the next gate. From the gate the path follows the river south for a further 1.3 km where you go through the next gate and turn right. Go down the small slope and through the wooden gate. The path now goes along the left-hand side of a field for a short distance until it reaches a footbridge between two gates.

Cross the footbridge and continue west, keeping to the right-hand side of a line of gnarled tree. As you proceed, you reach a bank on your left where there are two slate tablets bearing the inscription 'Uppingham School in grateful memory of 1876 and 1877'. Uppingham School is a prestigious boys' school in Rutland that suffered an epidemic of typhoid during the nineteenth century. The headmaster, Edward Thring, temporarily moved the entire school faculty to Borth to escape the disease, saving many young lives.

Shortly after the slate memorial tablets you will reach a lane and a church on higher ground on your left; this is St Matthew's church. As you pass the graveyard there are what appear to be small graves alongside the fence at the side of the lane: these graves belong to pets buried just outside the consecrated ground. Two of the most recent ones are 'Lucky I' buried in 2000 and 'Lucky II' buried in 2009. Will there be a 'Lucky III'?

Turn right on the lane and follow it north-west for 230 metres

*Petrified tree stumps . . . all that remains of the king's hunting forest*

to a railway crossing. Cross the line and turn right for a short distance. Just before you reach the station turn left along a lane that will lead you back to the seafront. Cross the road and turn right following the promenade north or, if you prefer, go down to the water's edge and walk along the beach. Dogs are, however, prohibited from this part of the beach in the town. If you have timed your walk along the beach when there is a low tide you will see a number of black objects near the waterline. These are fossilized tree stumps, all that is left of the great forest where Gwyddno used to hunt. A 2.5 km stroll along the beach will bring you back to the car park where the walk started.

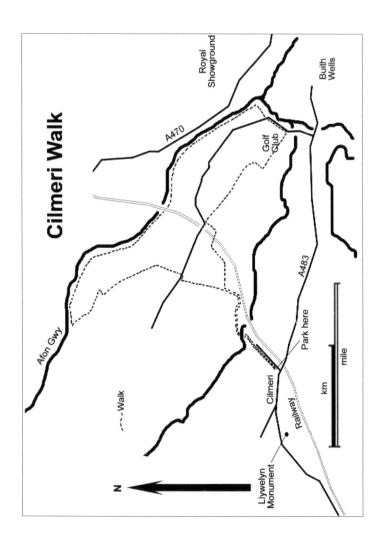

Cilmeri Walk

**4**

# *Llywelyn ein Llyw Olaf –*
# Llywelyn our Last Leader

Llywelyn the Great had united Wales. Welsh patriots called him Prince Llywelyn I of Wales. He ruled for forty years but, in 1240, he died. His sons began to squabble about who would replace him as ruler. It was the opportunity the English king, Henry III, had been waiting for. 'We will invade and crush the Welsh while they are arguing amongst themselves', he ordered.

The English army swept across north Wales. The Welsh princes, unprepared for a war, sued for peace.

'Lay down your arms and pay homage to me', demanded the king. The princes protested and Henry grew angry.

'You challenge my authority? I'll show you who is king. From this day forth, all your land east of the Conwy will become part of England, to be ruled by my son, Prince Edward. The people there are his vassals, to do with as he pleases', said the king.

'You cannot annex half our land and make it English', complained the Welsh princes.

'Take care or I will take all of your land', warned the king, and dismissed the Welsh princes.

'Your Majesty, we do not have enough soldiers to garrison all of Wales', warned one of the king's advisors.

King Henry considered the problem. He knew the Welsh princes would one day rise up against him if he did not do something. Then a plan came to him. 'Llywelyn has grandsons and they are his rightful heirs, are they not?' said the king.

'That is so, your majesty', replied an advisor.

'West Wales will be divided into three petty kingdoms. Each kingdom will pay homage to me and each will be ruled by one of Llywelyn's rightful heirs to the throne', commanded the king.

It was a final act of humiliation for the Welsh nobility.

As commanded by King Henry, Llywelyn the Great's grandsons were made the rulers of West Wales and the land was divided between three young princes, Llywelyn, Owain and Dafydd.

'Your majesty, why have you given the west of Wales to three young princes?' asked a minister.

'Watch and see. They are young and vain and will soon argue over their petty estates. They will turn on each other. Brother will battle brother and cousin conspire against cousin', replied the king.

Henry III's strategy worked. Young Dafydd conspired with his elder brother Owain and they turned on Llywelyn. Llywelyn gathered his men and met his brothers in battle at Bryn Derwin. He defeated Owain and Dafydd and captured them. It was a brilliant victory. 'Are we not all Welshmen here? Join me. Let us unite and take back what belongs to Wales', said Llywelyn, to his prisoners.

The patriotic appeal to his countrymen worked. The combined Welsh armies led by Llywelyn, Owain and Dafydd, turned east, crossed the Conwy and reclaimed Welsh land that had been stolen by the English Prince Edward. The men cheered Llywelyn as victory followed victory.

A messenger arrived at Llywelyn's camp. 'The English king wants peace', he cried.

'What are his terms?' asked Llywelyn.

'King Henry will recognise that you are the true Prince of Wales and allow you to keep all the land east of the Conwy that you have captured', said the messenger.

'That is generous of him. What does the king want in return?' inquired Llywelyn.

'The king is old and sick of war. All he asks in return is your tribute and yearly payment of 3,000 marks,' answered the messenger.

'His terms are fair. Tell King Henry that we accept them,' said Llywelyn. That night many toasts were drunk to Llywelyn, Prince of Wales.


A short time later bad news reached Wales. Henry III was dead. There was a new king on the throne of England: Henry's son Edward. Edward had been humiliated by Llywelyn and wanted revenge. He sent a secret message to Dafydd with an offer to make him Prince of Wales. 'Kill Llywelyn and I will make you the Prince of Wales.' It was a tempting proposition.

The three assassins listened to Dafydd carefully. 'When the deed is done, you are to ride East and speak to no one. Do you understand?' whispered Dafydd.

The men nodded. They left and rode towards Llywelyn's camp. Snow began to fall and before long a blizzard raged. The land turned white and the men's horses sank up to their flanks in the deep snow.

'We are lost', cried the murderers and abandoned their quest.

When King Edward heard the assassination had failed he vowed to deal with Prince Llywelyn himself, but he needed an excuse to invade Wales again. His chance came when Llywelyn failed to pay the yearly tribute promised to Edward's father.

Once more, an English army crossed the border into Wales. Dafydd, the deceitful brother, turned against Llywelyn and sided with the English king. Llywelyn's property was seized and, realising that he could not win, Llywelyn surrendered to the king.

'Why should I let you live?' said Edward to his captor.

'My liege. I swore loyalty to your father Henry and I am a honourable man. I have not broken my pledge', replied Llywelyn.

Edward recognised that Lywelyn had spoken the truth and granted his freedom. A period of peace followed during which Llywelyn fell in love with Eleanor, grandaughter of King John of England. Llywelyn and Eleanor married and the now impoverished Prince of Wales lived contentedly with his new bride.

'I am with child,' announced Eleanor one day. Llywelyn was overjoyed.

Then a rider bought news to Llywelyn's house. 'Your brother Dafydd has turned against King Edward,' said the rider.

'Why? He's been well rewarded by Edward', said Lywelyn.

'My Lord. Your brother Dafydd is a greedy man. He betrayed you once, hoping to win a kingdom and even now, as lord of the land east of the River Conwy, he thirsts for more', explained the messenger.

'Where is he?' asked Llywelyn.

'Dafydd has attacked Hawarden and massacred the English garrison. He marches on Rhuddlan. As we speak, the English King is preparing for war,' replied the messenger.

'I must help my brother,' said Llywelyn.

'My lord, Dafydd is your enemy. He sent assassins to kill you,' said the messenger.

'I know, but he is a Welshman and my brother,' replied Llywelyn.

Prince Llywelyn gathered his retainers together and marched south, to raise a new army. Once more, Welshmen flocked to his banner. As the army travelled, sad news reached Llywelyn. His wife

Eleanor had died giving birth to a daughter. The heartbroken prince named the child Gwenllian. By the time Llywelyn reached Builth Wells, his army was 7,000 strong. They stopped and camped at Cilmeri by the Irfon river.

An English army, led by the Marcher Lords Edward and Roger Mortimer, approached from the south. The armies lined up ready for battle. Only Afon Irfon separated the opposing forces.

A herald from the English army crossed the river under a flag of truce. 'My Lords Edward and Roger Mortimer want peace and offer terms to avoid giving battle today,' he cried.

'What are the terms?' called Prince Llywelyn.

'They wish to meet and talk with you,' replied the Herald.

Llywelyn and eighteen of his men went forward carrying a white flag. As they reached the river a great roar went up from the English. It was a trap. English archers had forded the river and sprang upon the Welsh army. A ferocious fight began. English heavy cavalry charged across the river straight towards Llywelyn. A lance struck the prince in the chest and he fell to the ground dead.

The Welsh soldiers fought on but, without their leader, the cause was lost and the English army won the day. After the battle Prince Lywelyn's head was cut from his body and sent to London where it was crowned with ivy to show that Llywelyn was nothing more than the 'King of the Outlaws'. The head was then set on a spike above the Tower of London gate, where it remained for the next fifteen years.

Having humiliated Llywelyn, King Edward also wanted to ensure that there would be no future heir left to claim the dead Llywelyn's legacy. He destroyed all the trappings of the Royal House of Gwynedd. Houses were looted. Royal plate was seized and melted down. Heraldic crests and royal records were destroyed. Llywelyn's treacherous brother, Dafydd, was hung drawn and quartered and his two young sons were incarcerated at Bristol Castle. Llywelyn's daughter Gwenllian was also seized and sent, together with Dafydd's daughters, to the remote Priory at Sempringham in Lincolnshire. None of the children was ever released and Gwenllian remained a prisoner, behind the high walls of the priory, for the next fifty-five years until she died.

In 1301 King Edward I invested his son Edward as the Prince of Wales, crowning him at Caernarfon. He was the first Englishman to be crowned a Prince of Wales. It was the final act of humiliation for the Welsh. The valiant patriot, Llywelyn, Lord of Snowdon, Prince of Wales and loyal brother, was the last Welshman to ever hold the title.

*'Near this place Llywelyn, our last leader, was killed, 1282'*

# Cilmeri Walk

This walk starts in the village of Cilmeri, a small village 2 miles west of Builth Wells (*Llanfair ym Muallt*) on the A483. It takes you across working farmland and through woodland towards the Wye (*Afon Gwy*) where you follow the river, meandering and tumbling through rock pools, on its way east. The Wye valley is surrounded by the Cambrian Mountains and there are great views to enjoy. Leaving the river, the walk continues across the golf course and back to Cilmeri. Some parts of the walk are badly signposted or not signposted at all, and there were features not shown on the Ordnance Survey map I used when I last did this walk. If you arrive from Builth Wells turn right, following a blue and white signpost to the 'Eglwys/Church'. As you turn, there is a bus shelter on the right with a parking area behind it. This is the starting point for the walk. The monument to Llywelyn is 600 metres further along the A483 on the left-hand side.

*Ordnance Survey map number 147 grid reference SO 007 514*
Latitude = 52.1523, Longitude = -3.4513
Lat = 52 degrees, 9.1 minutes North
Long = 3 degrees, 27.1 minutes West

| | |
|---|---|
| Length | 10.02 km – 6.22 miles |
| Maximum height | 195.26 metres |
| Minimum height | 125.11 metres |
| Height ascended | 258.75 metres |
| Navigation | Moderate |
| Difficulty | Moderate |
| Estimated time | 3 hours 57 minutes |

I have started the walk by the bus shelter simply to avoid walking along the main road. Builth Wells hosts the Royal Welsh Agricultural Show each July. It is a big and important event – the largest agricultural show in Europe – and expresses the richness and diversity of rural life in Wales. Typical attendance is over 200,000 people. The whole area becomes one giant campsite and is heaving with people determined to have fun. Unless you like the idea of walking along a riverbank crowded with tents and caravans I would suggest avoiding show week (but remember, various events are held there all year round). At other times this is a delightfully quiet walk with plenty to enjoy.

From the parking area, walk north-east along the lane. This will take you downhill with the single track railway line on your right. After 450 metres you reach a bridge where you turn left over Afon Ghwerfri, a tributary of the Wye. After the bridge the road becomes a track and turns right so that the river is on your right. Follow the track uphill to the farmyard, where you go straight on along the track with the house on your right and the main barns on your left.

The track now climbs and then bears right before descending towards a bridge under the railway line. Do not go under the railway. Instead turn left and continue along the track so that the railway is on your right. After 130 metres the track turns north, away from the railway line, and ascends for 140 metres to a metal gate. Ignore the stone track below the gate, which forks away to the left. Just above the gate a footpath joins from the right. It is from this path that you return on your way back to Cilmeri. Go through the gate and walk straight on, between the farmhouse and the barns, to a second gate leading to a road where you continue straight on. Follow the road as it continues north for another 320 metres to 'Rhos Cwym', a house on the corner of a T-junction. Turn right at the junction and follow the road south-east for 20 metres to a bridleway sign pointing to the left, where you leave the road.

The pathway now follows the left-hand edge of a pretty

*Monument to Prince Llywelyn.*
*People still leave flowers in his memory*

wooded valley. After 250 metres the path begins to bear left so that you are walking slightly west of north. Another 100 metres brings you to a fork in the path where you keep left, ignoring the path downhill to the right. From here the bridleway starts to descend and you go further into the wood for another 240 metres, to the next junction, where you go straight on taking the right-hand path.

Continue downhill through the wood for a further 320 metres, until you reach a wire fence directly ahead, where you turn right so that the fence is on your left. Follow the fence line 70 metres to a lane, where you turn left. You now leave the wood as the lane takes you north-west for 450 metres, passing Dolyrerw Farm on your right, to a cattle grid. Just before the cattle grid, turn sharp right and leave the lane through a gate leading to a field. The Wye will now be on your left and you have joined the 'Wye Valley Walk' footpath. From here you have a flat stroll along the side of the Wye for the next 3.2 km. To start with, the river is flowing quite quickly. After 200 metres you reach 'Plum Tree Pool' – an evocative name, but I could find no sign of a plum tree.

Walk along the side of the river through four more gates leading from field to field. As you continue through the last field the pace of the river slows and the field narrows while the path begins to climb into woodland and to a metal kissing gate. Go through the gate and walk along the path through the wood. The path descends to take you under a railway bridge that spans the river, and then it climbs so that you are high above the river, which is placid and still. You now have a pleasant 750 metres walk through the woods. As you continue, the sound of the river grows louder as the water picks up speed, and you pass points along the river where planks have been placed precariously between the rocks by fishermen eager to reach the better fish runs.

As you leave the woods there is a large and very fast pool in the river next to a gate leading to a field. Go through the gate and continue along the riverbank for a further 800 metres until you reach the corner of the field, with no way ahead. This is where the tributary you crossed earlier joins the Wye. From here, if you look north-east across the river, you will see the Royal Showground. At the end of the field, turn right and follow the boundary south-west for 170 metres until you reach a gate leading to a road.

Walk 250 metres straight on along the road, past Builth Wells Golf Club, to a footpath sign on the right, which you follow. This takes you across the golf course along a tree-lined avenue between the fairways and gives you the opportunity to observe the hitters and hackers as they play their rounds. Be wary, since ramblers are invisible to golfers and stray balls can be dangerous.

Leave the golf course with the 18th tee on your left. From here the footpath continues into a wood. Do not, however, go straight on. The path you need to take turns right and goes around the perimeter of the wood. This turning is poorly signposted with one small yellow arrow and, because the path is small, it is easy to miss. The path around the wood can be overgrown and difficult to follow but the general rule is to keep the wire fence and the golf course on your right. Follow the fence line until you arrive at a stile, which you cross.

From the stile walk a short distance to the next stile keeping the fence on your left. From here you cross a garden with a large house and pond on your right. Three more stiles follow as you continue walking north-west. The pathway here is very narrow in places. The third stile brings you to a field. Walk north-west across the field so that you pass a lake on your left. The lake is a recent creation and, at the time of writing, is not on any Ordnance Survey map. You are aiming for a stile in the fence beyond the lake. Go over this stile into the next field and keep walking north-west, uphill, towards the large metal gate in the far corner. There is a distinct lack of signage during this part of the walk. The footpath is indicated here by a small piece of yellow sticky tape on the gate.

Ahead of you is a tarmac driveway, again a recent creation, not shown on the maps. Cross the drive, go through the gate opposite and continue, keeping to the right-hand side of the field, until you reach a stile. Cross the stile and the railway line – remembering to look, since the track is still in use – to the next stile leading to a field. Walk west, up the slope to another stile, which leads to a lane. Ignore the stile on the opposite side of the lane.

Turn left and continue along the lane, passing a house on your right. Just after the house the footpath turns right and follows the right-hand side of a field, down hill, to the next stile. Cross the stile into the next field, continue walking west and keeping near the top of the field to the last stile of the walk.

Cross the stile and turn left to rejoin the track leading to Rhosterig Farm that you walked up earlier. From here you walk down hill and back through the farmyard, retracing your steps to Cilmeri.

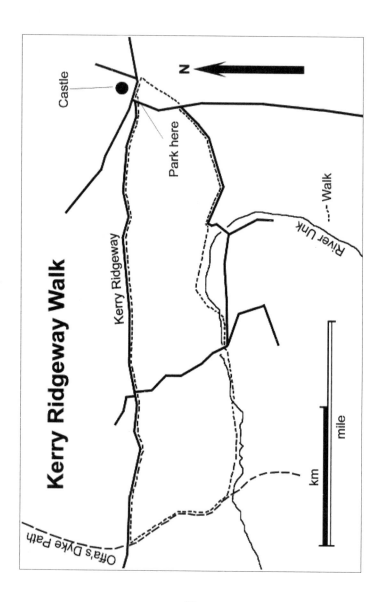

Kerry Ridgeway Walk

Castle

Park here

Kerry Ridgeway

N

River Unk

--- Walk

Offa's Dyke Path

km    mile

## 5

# The Drovers

Before the invention of the railway, the wealth of Wales walked slowly to England. Records show that in one year in the eighteenth century 9,000 cattle swam across the Menai Straits from Anglesey and were driven to England. 6,000 left from Llŷn peninsula and 30,000 from central Wales. William Brooke, in *The True causes of our Present Distress for Provisions* (1800), estimated that in 1798 a total of 600 million pounds of beef were consumed in England. English yeomanry ate Welsh beef while Welsh farmers lived on a meagre diet of barley and potatoes. A Pembrokeshire farm labourer's grace tells the story:

*Arglwydd annwyl! Dyma Fwyd*
*Cawl sur a bara llwyd.*

[Good Lord! What a spread –
Sour broth and mouldy bread.]

To protect the cattle's hooves on the long walk they were shod with narrow metal shoes that were nailed on. A thrower, or feller, would pass a rope over each beast and loop it around the legs. Then he would topple the animal by the horns and tie it, allowing a blacksmith and his lad to shoe the animal. It needed great strength and the team of men would shoe between sixty and seventy cattle in a day.

It wasn't only cattle that walked to distant markets. Flocks of geese would be walked through wet tar and sand to coat their webbed feet ready for the journey. Pigs were dressed with leather-soled woollen socks.

The drovers that took the animals to the markets of England were tough men. Droving paid well but it was a dangerous job. Wolves, robbers and cut-throats roamed the countryside. Drovers undertook financial errands on behalf of farmers, paying absentee landlords. On 10 April 1734 a Mr. Bulkeley wrote to Thomas Lewis, a drover, instructing him to use £15, from the sale of animals in London, to pay for his son's keep as an apprentice lawyer in Chancery Lane. Travellers joined the drovers for protection. In 1853 Mrs Jane Evans from Pumsaint, near Lampeter, was allegedly the first woman to travel with the drovers, when she went to join Florence Nightingale's nursing mission to the Crimean War.

Drovers handled large sums of money and a banking system grew up around the business. It is recorded that, in 1806, drovers David Roberts and Griffith Jones arrived at the cattle fairs in Kent and sold their herd for the handsome sum of £6,053. Banks in Llandeilo issued their own promissory notes and Lloyds Bank began life serving the drovers of Wales. The Aberystwyth and Tregaron Bank, often called the Black Sheep Bank, started as a drovers' bank. The values of its £1–£10 notes were illustrated by numbers of sheep, while the 10 shilling note had a smaller picture of a single sheep. Drovers transported gold to be sold in London for the miners of Rhaeader, agreeing to split profits.

The responsibility of transporting animals to England, and money back to Wales, was based largely on trust, but the industry was regulated by the state. Drovers had to be over thirty years old, married, and own a house before they could be licensed. When applying for a licence the drovers would always describe their work as 'An art and a mystery'. Anyone caught droving without a licence could be fined £5 and imprisoned for vagrancy. To stop drovers defaulting on their customers Queen Anne passed a law prohibiting drovers from declaring themselves bankrupt to avoid repaying money in their care. Droving was not allowed on Sundays. In 1869 a drover was fined £1 plus 8/6d (42.5 pence) costs for driving swine through Builth Wells on the Sabbath.

Drovers were the main carriers of news to the people. It was a drover that first bought Wales news of the British victory at Waterloo in 1815.

Using the turnpike road system was expensive. Heavy toll charges for moving the animals made them uneconomical for many drovers, while others were willing to pay the tolls in order to reach the cattle fairs more quickly and with the animals in better condition so they would fetch a higher price. Mostly, however, the drovers used ancient tracks and high roads where the animals could graze as they moved and the tolls avoided. Many of the drovers' routes still exist, while others have vanished, becoming part of our network of trunk roads.

During the civil war, landowners of north Wales wrote to the king of England asking for protection for the herds being moved. The war made droving a particularly dangerous business. In 1645 parliamentary soldiers seized nearly 1000 beasts from a party of eighteen drovers and no compensation was paid.

Welsh black cattle are a hardy breed and ideal for droving. They can survive on poor pasture and are nimble enough to climb mountain tracks. There were frequent inns and cider houses along the drovers' routes. These important places of refreshment were often signposted by three Scots pines, positioned to be visible from miles away. Each night the animals were corralled in a field for half a penny per beast. These 'halfpenny fields' are still greener and lusher than the surrounding land because of the manure left by so many animals. The head drover, known as the porthmon, would sleep in the inn, while the junior drovers would sleep by the animals. Often the inn would have a blacksmith ready to repair broken shoes.

Travelling at a steady two miles an hour, a drive from north Wales to London would take three weeks. The cry 'Heiptrw ho' could be heard for miles, warning the farmers ahead to secure their animals so they did not become mixed with the moving herd. Corgis were used to drive the stock: these intelligent dogs were low enough to avoid getting kicked by the cattle as they did their work. Returning after the drive, the dogs would often go ahead of their masters, arriving home a day or two before the men.

Drover Robert Jones kept accounts of bringing sheep from Carmarthenshire to London through Pinner and Edgware between 1823 and 1837. Pigs made a similar journey travelling at a steady six miles per day.

The drovers of Monmouthshire would congregate at 'Two Tumps' on the western end of the Kerry Ridgeway with their animals, ready to start their drive along the oldest road in Wales.

While it was a tough business, some of the drovers were educated men. Edward Morus was a famous poet who continued as a drover until he was eighty-two, when he died and was buried in Essex. Others grew wealthy from the trade. When part-time drover Rowland Edmund died in 1819, his will included £963 plus sheep, cattle, pigs and horses amounting to a considerable fortune. He was buried in a cemetery near Harlech Castle.

Finally, with the coming of the railways, droving went into decline. It was easier and quicker to move the animals by train and they arrived in better condition. Droving did not die out completely. During the 1914–1918 war cattle were again walked from Wales to England. One of the last drovers, Morris Roberts, finally retired in the 1930s and became a farmer, ending a proud tradition that had lasted for over a thousand years.

# Kerry Ridgeway Walk

The Kerry Ridgeway is one of the oldest drovers' routes across the Cambrian Mountains. The Ridgeway runs for fifteen miles, from Cider House Farm, Powys, in the west, to Bishop's Castle, Shropshire (*Sir Amwythig*), in the east. The ridge seldom drops below 1000 feet and there are superb views of up to 70 miles depending on the weather. Our circular walk starts at Bishop's Moat, where a Motte and Bailey castle once stood guarding the track. From there you walk south and follow the strangely named River Unk through Shropshire before turning north, along a section of Offa's Dyke, climbing back to the Ridgeway and into Wales. The last part of the walk is an easy two-mile stroll along the Ridgeway, following the same route the drovers used centuries ago. Bishop's Moat is 12 miles east of Newtown (*Y Drenewydd*), 10.5 miles north of Knighton (*Trefyclo*) and 2.1 miles west of Bishop's Castle. It is possible to park on the grass verge at the road junction beside the ruined castle. It is a remote spot and there are no toilets or other facilities along the walk.

*Ordnance Survey map number 137 grid reference SO 290 896*
Latitude = 52.4995, Longitude = -3.0474
Lat = 52 degrees, 30.0 minutes North
Long = 3 degrees, 2.8 minutes West

| | |
|---|---|
| Length | 7.71 km – 4.79 miles |
| Maximum height | 391.17 metres |
| Minimum height | 284.82 metres |
| Height ascended | 181.92 metres |
| Navigation | Easy |
| Difficulty | Easy |
| Estimated time | 2 hours 59 minutes |

Leave the car and walk east along the lane so that the castle mound is on your left. The castle was built around 1120 by the Bishop of Hereford and originally had a bailey that was 100 metres by 65 metres, demonstrating the importance of the Kerry Ridgeway in ancient times. It is believed that the Kerry Ridgeway is older than the Dark Age and Iron Age earthworks that lie nearby, and there are Bronze Age burials and a stone circle near the ridge.

Follow the lane for 150 metres, until you reach a metal gate and footpath sign on your right. Leave the lane along the footpath, which crosses the field in a southwesterly direction. As you cross the field, aim for the house in the far corner. At the corner of the field, take the right-hand gate leading to a lane, and continue south-west along the lane so that you pass the house on your left. The lane takes you downhill for 300 metres into a pretty valley. It then bears right as you follow the lane along the valley.

After a further 660 metres you reach a sharp left-hand turn and a pair of white houses on the corner. Leave the lane here and follow the footpath sign straight ahead so that the houses are on your right. Go through the metal gate into a field and continue walking west so that the river is on your left. This is the River Unk, a tributary of the River Clun.

Walk for 300 metres to a stile leading into a small conifer wood and a second stile leading to the next field where you continue following the river to a track and a shallow ford. Cross the river and go through the metal gate into the farmyard, continuing straight ahead up the yard. At the top of the yard turn right, walking west along the lane, through a metal gate and past a house on your right. After 230 metres along the lane, you reach a junction, where you leave the lane following the footpath sign pointing through a metal gate into a field that is straight ahead.

*Walking west towards the Unk*

The footpath forks here and you take the right-hand path along the valley.

Continue for 200 metres to a stile leading to the next field, where you continue straight on, keeping the river on your right. Keep walking west for another 750 metres until you reach a junction with a footpath marked by yellow way-markers and white acorns. This is the Offa's Dyke Path that runs south to north and is a popular walkers' route. King Offa built the dyke as a defensive barrier against the Welsh in the eighth century, and the walk, which is 177 miles long, was opened in 1971.

Turn right and walk along the path on Offa's Dyke, over a footbridge crossing the River Unk and turn left following a track uphill for a short distance to a stile on your right. Cross the stile and follow the Offa's Dyke sign pointing uphill through the wood. When you come to a crossroads in the paths, continue straight

*Walking a section of Offa's Dyke*

*Kerry Ridgeway: once a busy trade route, but now a quiet country lane*

on, ignoring the blue way-markers. At the top of the climb the path emerges from the wood and you cross a stile into a field. Walk along the left-hand side of the field to the next stile, where the path continues between a fence on your right and the earth remains of the original dyke on your left. There are a number of large burrows in the dyke, suggesting that badgers have taken up residence.

Keep walking along the path until you reach two wooden gates leading to a tarmac lane. The second gate is the border and you have just passed from Shropshire into Powys. You are now standing on the Kerry Ridgeway, which dissects the Offa's Dyke Path. Turn right along the Ridgeway so that you are walking east, in the same direction that the drovers would herd their animals. Kerry Ridgeway was last used for droving about 150 years ago, after which railways made the practice of walking animals to England uneconomic.

Typically, drovers' routes were about 14 feet wide, so the stock had room to move and the animals could find some grazing. Although the Kerry Ridgeway is now a metalled single-track lane, there is very little traffic and the original size of the track is clearly visible.

Continue walking east along the Ridgeway and look north where you will see a strange group of four hills. These are the hills of Churchstoke (*Yr Ystog*). According to a passing walker they are also known as the 'Devil's Chair', because according to folklore the Devil always sits there to rest when the hills are hidden by cloud.

Further on the lane descends and you pass 'Dog and Duck Cottage' on your left. The Ridgeway then climbs again, and after a further 2.1 km you arrive back at the starting point of the walk.

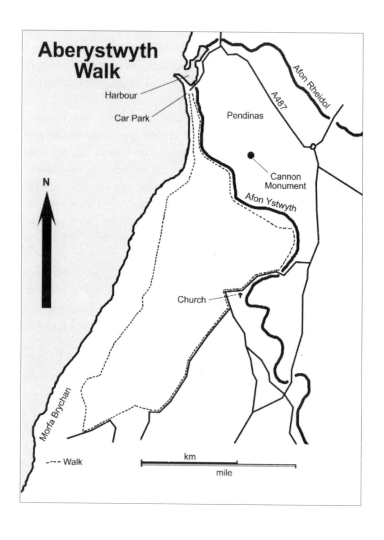

Aberystwyth Walk

Harbour

Car Park

Pendinas

Afon Rheidol

A487

Cannon Monument

Afon Ystwyth

N

Church

Morfa Brychan

- - - Walk

km

mile

# 6

# The Headless Dog

Maelor Mawr (or Maelor the giant) lived in a time before history. His home was Dinas Maelor a fort, high on a hill. From there, Maelor would look down on Afon Ystwyth and the sea beyond. Today we call his home Pen Dinas.

Maelor had three sons Cornippyn, Crygyn and Bwba, and all were giants and fearless warriors.

One day, out hunting Maelor, was surprised by his enemies. They had watched and waited until he was alone. Fifty men surrounded Maelor, but he did not yield. He drew back his bow and struck one with an arrow, killing him instantly. A second fell and then a third. Undeterred, Maelor's enemies drew closer, for they hated him and had sworn to kill him.

With no arrows left, Maelor threw down his bow and snatched up his sword. He swung left and right with all his strength. He slashed and cut, hacked and sliced. The battle raged for hours, but there were too many enemy warriors and, worn out by the battle, Maelor fell to his knees. Attackers' bodies lay all around. Maelor had extracted a terrible price for his defeat. His captors beat him cruelly and bound him hand and foot.

'Let's kill him now,' cried one. 'We'll hang him from that tree.'

'Enough of this,' the leader cried. 'He deserves a better death. He fought a valiant fight.'

They left him tied for hours and debated what to do.

'We have decided what would be fair. Before you die you are

allowed one wish,' said the leader, at long last.

'If I must die, there is one thing that I would like to do,' whispered Maelor, 'to blow my horn just three times, before I give my final gasp.'

'Fetch his hunting horn,' the leader said, and gave it to Maelor. He then cut Maelor's bonds.

Maelor took a mighty breath and blew with all his strength. He puffed so hard that a thunderous blast that blew out all his hair. Undeterred by his naked brow Maelor tried again. A second blast came from his horn, much stronger than the last. When it was done his fingers and his toes had parted and flown off. The final call the horn made was louder than before. The horn thundered one more time, shattered into pieces and lay there on the floor. Maelor looked triumphantly and he waited for his end. It did not come quickly. They could not kill him yet. His captors were all writhing, their eardrums burst and red. The blood ran down their tunics as they screamed in pain and dread.

The hunting horn had done its work and roused Cornippyn from his slumber. Hearing his father's cry for help, he grabbed a horse, leashed his faithful hound and set off to the rescue. Cornippyn galloped hard toward the sound he had heard coming from the far side of the river. His spurs dug deep, driving the horse on towards the running water. Faster still they had to go, to jump across the river. The faithful hound could not keep up with such a furious chase. The leash went tight and like a whip it cracked – before the line went slack. The dog was gone, its head pulled off and dropped into the Ystwyth.

Cornippyn rode on and joined the fight but his efforts were in vain. He could not stop his father's death, despite a furious struggle. He died as well that very day, a victim of his blunder. The other brothers joined the fight and they were slain as well. The only one that was left was the faithful hound, still paddling in the river. He clambered out, shook himself and thought of walking home. Then, he wondered where his head had gone and trotted off to find it.

Today, locals speak of seeing a headless dog wandering the fields of Pen Dinas, searching for its head. Others say it appears beside the beds of sick children and guards them from evil.

*Follow the footpath north alongside the Ystwyth*

# Aberystwyth Walk

The university town of Aberystwyth, considered by many to be the capital of central Wales, is a bustling place popular with holidaymakers eager to explore the Victorian promenade, the medieval castle and the marina. Our walk leaves from a quieter car park beside the Ystwyth and follows it south as it meanders towards Llanfarian. The walk then climbs south-west along narrow lanes and turns west before returning along the coast path. You will be rewarded with good views of Cardigan Bay and of the town stretched out below you. There is some climbing involved and the

**Ordnance Survey map number 135 grid reference SN 579 806**
Latitude = 52.4055, Longitude = -4.0896
Lat = 52 degrees, 24.3 minutes North
Long = 4 degrees, 5.4 minutes West

| | |
|---|---|
| Length | 9.47 km – 5.88 miles |
| Maximum height | 145.18m |
| Minimum height | 2.19m |
| Height ascended | 288.61m |
| Navigation | Easy |
| Difficulty | Moderate |
| Estimated time | 3 hours 53 minutes |

last part of the walk, returning you to the beach, is steep, so it may be slippery if the ground is wet. Aberystwyth is 14 miles north of Aberaeron on the A487 and 16 miles south of Machynlleth, again on the A487, or you can approach it from the east along the A44. The free car park is at the southern end of the town near the marina. Drive along Penparcau Road and look for a road called Pen-yr-Angor. Follow it to the beach where you will find the car park. There are no toilet facilities at the car park but there are public toilets at the top of Penparcau Road where it joins the A487.

Leave the car park and walk south, away from the harbour, following the footpath beside the river. The beach on your right was a popular landing place for smugglers, who then ferried their contraband in small boats along the Ystwyth to Llanfarian. From there the tobacco, brandy and even salt were distributed far and wide by drovers. It was a big business, controlled by two local families, and although there were excise men in Aberystwyth it is probable they were paid to look the other way. The hill on your left is Pen Dinas, where one of the largest prehistoric hill forts in Wales has been excavated. The tower that you can see, designed to look like an upturned cannon, is a monument erected to commemorate a local man who was one of the Duke of Wellington's officers at the battle of Waterloo when the French were defeated.

After 600 metres there is a kissing gate where you bear left, continuing to follow the river south-east for 400 metres. The path then turns south for 250 metres and then south-east once more. Keep following the riverbank for the next 1.3 km until you arrive at a metal kissing gate leading to a lane. Go straight on through the gate and walk south-west along the lane for 600 m, passing Eglwys Llanychaearn, a pretty church on your right. Follow the lane as it turns to the left and after another 130 m turn right along the lane signposted to 'Morfa Bychan Holiday Park'. The walk now takes you south-west for 1.5 km until you reach a sharp left turn in the lane and a stile leading to the right. Cross the stile and walk west across the field with the hedge on your left. Where the hedge ends turn left and walk downhill, aiming for the sea and the lowest part of the field.

When you reach the fence, go over the next stile and continue

*Aberystwyth harbour*

*Looking south from the car park.*
*The return route descends along the ridge on the left*

downhill in the same direction until you reach a stile leading to a road. Follow the road downhill over the cattle grid. Continue along the road for 300 metres to a gate on your right signposted 'Coastal Path, Aberystwyth 3 miles'. Go through the gate and follow the footpath north across the gorse and bracken covered grass. Below you, on your left, is Morfa Bychan Holiday Park.

The path climbs for 130 metres to the next signpost where you continue the walk, following the direction of the signpost slightly downhill. This will bring you to a stile where the path descends for a short distance before turning to the right and climbing again. Continue on for 200 metres to the next stile where the path turns to the left and you walk north-east for another 340 metres to the next stile.

From here you continue to climb north-east. After 280 metres Aberystwyth comes into view ahead of you and the harbour, castle and promenade can all be seen. The structure between the castle and the sea is a war memorial designed by Italian Mario Rutelli and represents the Angel of Peace emerging from the end of the First World War. A new marina was built in the harbour in 1995 at a cost of £9m.

In the distance above the town you will see a railway going up the cliff to a strange building. This is a Camera Obscura, a recreation of a Victorian attraction where visitors can stand and view 1000 square miles of land and sea.

Keep following the coastal path for 500 metres to a group of two stiles where the path turns left and then descends past strange rock formations. Continuing north, you climb to the top of a ridge and the most spectacular part of the walk. At the end of the ridge, the path descends down to the beach where you continue north, following the curve of the sand for 1.2 km, back to the car park.

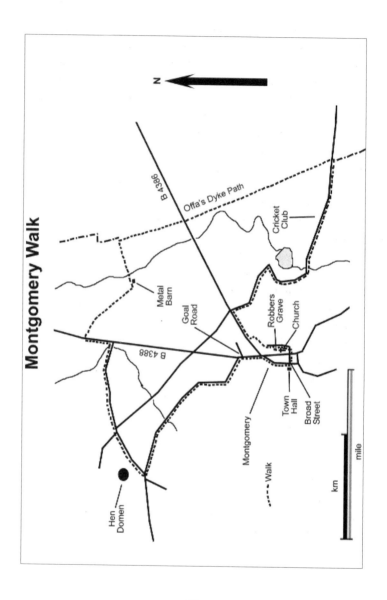

Montgomery Walk

N

B 4386

Offa's Dyke Path

Cricket Club

Metal Barn

Goal Road

Robbers Grave

Church

B 4388

Town Hall

Broad Street

Montgomery

Walk

Hen Domen

km

mile

**7**

# The Robber's Grave

In the early 1800s Montgomery was a thriving market town. A plaque on Broad Street tells us that in 1840 over fifty tradesmen were based in the town including two blacksmiths, five bakers, three cobblers, three butchers, three carpenters, three coopers, eight grocers, two seedsmen, four drapers, four maltsters, two plumbers, two masons, three saddlers, two tailors, one bricklayer, one brazier, one timber merchant, one tanner, one currier (a person who prepares tanned leather for a saddler or cobbler), one clockmaker, one bookseller and one scrivener (a professional reader and writer, sometimes employed to write letters for those who could not).

When John Davies, a plasterer from Wrexham, found himself out of work in 1819, he travelled to Montgomery looking for work where he gained employment as a *gwas* (farm servant) working for Mrs Morris, a widow. Mrs Morris lived with her daughter Jane and, since the death of her husband, the farm had become neglected and run-down. Creditors, including a local tradesman, Thomas Pearce, were watching eagerly, hoping to obtain the farm at a knock-down price.

Mrs Morris was relieved to employ Davies. She knew she could not run the farm without a man to do the heavy work. John Davies was a quiet, taciturn individual who kept himself to himself, but he was strong and a hard worker. Robert Parker, a local quarryman, was a regular visitor to the farm and was engaged to Mrs Morris' daughter Jane. He eyed the new farm servant labourer living at the farm as a threat and took an instant dislike to Davies.

Davies was good with the animals and he quickly improved the quality of the stock, getting good prices for them at the market. Before long Davies' hard work made a difference to the farm and Mrs Morris' fortunes started to improve. The daughter, Jane, grew to like the quiet young labourer. Sensing that he was losing her, Parker became aggressive and one evening the two men came to blows.

When Davies returned to the farm, Jane bathed his cut face but he would say nothing of how he became injured. Later, when a friend told the young woman about the fight, she realised that Parker was a bully and that she did not want to marry him. She broke off the engagement, leaving Robert Parker a bitter man, intent on revenge.

The tradesman, Pearce, was also bitter as he watched Davies' effort to improve the farm and saw his opportunity for some easy money slipping from his grasp. One evening Pearce and Parker met in the taproom of a public house and, after several drinks, hatched a plan to get rid of John Davies for good.

The following day Pearce staggered into town with a bloody head.

'Help me,' he moaned. 'I've been robbed.'

A crowd quickly gathered around the stricken man.

'Tell us, what happened?' they cried.

'I was riding along the road at Hendomen. When I got to the crossroads a ruffian attacked me and beat me about the head with a cudgel,' he whimpered.

'Did you see who it was that attacked you?' asked the crowd.

'No, but he stole my money, six guineas and my gold watch,' answered Pearce with a sly grin.

A hue and cry began and the magistrate's men combed the

*The Robber's Grave, in St Nicholas' churchyard, Montgomery.*
*A sad memorial for an innocent man*

countryside looking for the highway robber, but there was no trace of the villain.

Later, unaware of the manhunt, John Davies came to market. It was busy on Broad Street with buyers and sellers enjoying the banter of quick business. The lambs Davies had bought from the farm sold for a good price and he went to the tavern to refresh himself before the long walk back to the farm. He saw Parker at the bar and turned to leave.

'Don't go. Come let us end our argument with a drink and behave like civil men,' called his adversary.

Davies looked at his enemy with distrust.

'Why should I drink with you?' he asked.

'I want to apologise for my temper. Here take a glass of beer with me and let us be friends. Landlord, another tankard if you please,' commanded Parker, and beckoned the farm servant to join him.

The two men stood at the bar and drank. Davies was unaware of the danger he was in. A few minutes later Parker's accomplice Pearce arrived and, spying the pair, let out a shriek.

'That's him, the man that beat me to the ground and stole my money and my watch,' he yelled and pointed at Davies.

The unfortunate farm servant was grabbed and searched. His drinking companion of moment's earlier thrust his bulging hand into Davies pocket and gave a triumphant yell.

'Here, what's this in his coat pocket?' He pulled out his hand and revealed six golden coins.

'That's my money,' cried Pearce.

'There's something else in the pocket,' said Parker with an evil leer. He thrust his hand in once more and produced the final proof.

'My gold watch! Fetch the constable. This villain must go before the magistrate,' called Pearce.

John Davies was taken to the jail on Gaol Street and kept in chains in the underground cell until his trial.

The Quarter Sessions were held in the Town Hall. Davies had no money to pay for a lawyer and conducted his own defence. The evidence against him was strong. The tavern was crowded when the stolen goods were found in his pocket and all swore to his guilt, unaware that Parker had placed the money and watch into the pocket of the unfortunate man. Davies protested his innocence throughout but his pleas fell on deaf ears. Highway robbery was a capital offence and he was quickly convicted of the crime he knew he did not commit.

The day of the execution arrived. It was cold and a great storm raged. A piercing wind blew from the north and sleet soaked the waiting crowd as they looked up at the noose.

'Have you anything to say before sentence is carried out?' said the hangman as the condemned man stood on the gallows with the rope about his neck.

The condemned man replied:

> I have been ill judged by man but am innocent of any crime. I curse my enemies for this foul deed and offer my soul to God for his honest judgement. If I am innocent in his court I tell you this; no grass will grow on my grave for 100 years so people, in years to come, will remember this evil injustice against John Davies, an honest fellow.

The trap door opened and John Davies dropped to his death.

He was buried in unconsecrated ground outside the churchyard at St Nicholas Church in 1821 and, for over 100 years, no grass grew on the grave. It is still there today and, although the grass has finally started to grow back, it still reminds us of when an honest man was unjustly hung and buried in a robber's grave.

*The walk takes you through the Lymore Estate*

# Montgomery Walk

Montgomery (*Trefaldwyn*) is a pretty, unspoilt, market town nestling on the border with England. It is on the B4385, 8 miles north east of Newtown and 7 miles south of Welshpool (*Y Trallwng*). Once an important transport link between the countries of England and Wales, the history of the town is reflected in its buildings, which retain their character. There is free car parking on Broad Street and public toilets, behind the Town Hall, at the end of Broad Street.

Our walk starts on Broad Street, where livestock markets were once held, takes you through St Nicholas' Churchyard, past 'The Robber's Grave' and then east to a section of Offa's Dyke where it turns north following the Dyke before returning to Montgomery through the hamlet of Hendomen. During the walk you cross the border between England and Wales four times.

**Ordnance Survey map number 137 grid reference SO 222 964**
Latitude = 52.5603, Longitude = -3.1482
Lat = 52 degrees, 33.6 minutes North
Long = 3 degrees, 8.9 minutes West

| | |
|---|---|
| Length | 10.01 km – 6.22 miles. |
| Maximum height | 173.29m |
| Minimum height | 86.00m |
| Height ascended | 209.36m |
| Navigation | Easy |
| Difficulty | Easy |
| Estimated time | 3 hour 20 minutes |

Having parked, you may choose to walk around Broad Street looking for several plaques mounted on different buildings. These give some of the history of the town. John Davies would have sold his animals here and the large building across the western end of the street is the Town Hall. It is here that the Quarter Sessions were held and where Davies would have been tried for his 'crime'.

Walk east along Broad Street, away from the Town Hall. Cross Bishop's Castle Street and walk along Church Bank to the gateway leading into the churchyard on your left. This is St Nicholas' church. Enter the churchyard and walk around the church to the north end of the churchyard. The 'robber's grave' lies on the left of the path near the north gate as you look away from the church' and is marked with a simple wooden cross. When Davies was buried this ground was unconsecrated, but the churchyard has since been enlarged.

Leave the churchyard through the north gate, turn right and then left onto the road where you walk downhill, along Church Bank and past the school. Just after the school the road becomes a path and continues downhill until you turn left past some cottages and emerge at a road. Turn right and follow the road for 250 m, where you turn right into a lane just before the national speed limit signs. Walk south along the lane for 200 m where it bears left and takes you south-east. After a further 250 m, you reach a cattle grid. Continue straight on over the cattle grid heading towards a lake. Continue south-east for another 150 m until the lane turns right and takes you in a circular line around the south side of the lake. This is part of the Lymore Estate, the history of which can be traced back to the Norman Conquest and is considered to have unique historic and geographic importance.

Go across the next cattle grid on the south-west side of the lake and continue along the lane as it passes farm buildings and a large empty pond on your right before continuing east. A short distance further on you pass Montgomery Cricket Club on your left and walk on through mature parkland for 420 m to a cattle grid where the lane enters woodland.

Continue east though the wood for 330 m until you reach the

next cattle grid and the lane leaves the wood. Go over the cattle grid, into Shropshire, and turn left, following the Offa's Dyke signpost to River Camlad 2¼ miles.

The next part of the walk is a 2.16 km stroll along the Offa's Dyke path as it takes you north. This section starts by following a hedge on your left for 762 m during which you cross three stiles. To the east, beyond Shropshire, are the hills of Lan Fawr and Corndon, both of which, because of the strange shape of the border, are in Wales. At the third stile the footpath crosses back into Wales and you continue in the same direction, but with the hedge on your right. From here you have good views of St Nicholas' Church and the ruin of Montgomery Castle on your left. After a further 316 m another stile takes you back into England. As you keep walking north parts of King Offa's medieval earthworks can be clearly seen on your right. Walking another 90 m brings you to the next stile, where the path continues downhill in the same direction with the dyke on your right.

Once you get to the bottom of the hill, go through the metal gate leading to a road. Cross the road and go through the gate leading to a track, which you follow, keeping the hedge on your right. Continue north for 700 m until you reach a point where the Offa's Dyke path turns right and the track turns left and goes west. Turn left and walk west along the track for 470 m to a metal barn.

Just after the barn, the track bears right and takes you north-west for 660 m until you reach a metal gate leading to a road. Turn left along the road for 210 m and then turn right, along the lane, immediately after 'Toll Cottage', a timber-framed house on the right. Walk uphill along the lane for the next 1.33 km. This takes you through the hamlet of Hendomen and, at the top of the hill, you pass a mound on your right from which the name Hendomen originates. This is all that remains of Hen Domen, a motte-and-bailey Castle, built by Roger De Montgomery in 1070. It was replaced by the newer stone castle built above the town in 1223.

Continue on past the mound for 300 m until you reach a road. The claimed attack and robbery on Thomas Pearce allegedly took place here. If you look south from here you will see a monument on the hill in the distance. This is Montgomery war memorial, located on the trig point on Town Hill, commemorating the dead of the first and second world wars. Turn left along the road so that you are walking south-east and continue along the road for 1.5 km as it brings you back to the town and passes beneath the castle on your right. As you enter the town you pass Old Gaol Road on your left. A plaque on the first building tells that, in 1740, it was the site of the town jail and included a dank underground cell where prisoners were kept in chains and where John Davies waited for his trial.

Pass Old Gaol Road and walk uphill for 220 m to a junction where you bear right, following the sign to the castle, toilets and the museum. The museum is on the right just before the town hall and contains a model of Roger De Montgomery's castle plus other interesting local information. From the museum you have just a few steps back to your car.

*Looking east, into England, from Offa's Dyke*

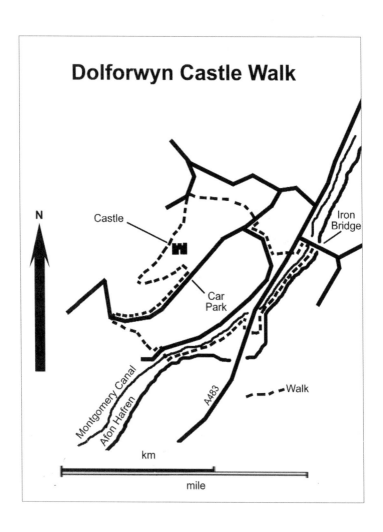

# Dolforwyn Castle Walk

Castle

Iron Bridge

Car Park

Montgomery Canal

Afon Hafren

A483

Walk

km

mile

# 8

# The Drowning of Hafren

There was a time when the Celtic nation covered the whole of Britain, and one ruler, named Locrinus, ruled over what is called England today. Invaders from the east were threatening the kingdom, and there were constant skirmishes. A fleet of Saxons, led by Humber the Hun, arrived, and the King's brother died in the battle that followed.

When King Locrinus learned that his brother was dead he vowed revenge on Humber. His family honour demanded it, and the protection of his Celtic realm made it inevitable. The Angles and Saxons had been threatening to invade for some time. Locrinus gathered his army and travelled east, to war. The two armies met near a mighty river and Locrinus killed his enemy. Humber had fought valiantly to the death and, recognising the bravery of his foe, King Locrinus named the river in honour of his enemy.

Following the battle Locrinus plundered the captured ships of his enemy, seizing gold, silver and prisoners. He divided the gold and silver amongst his victorious army, and sold the prisoners into serfdom – all, that is, except one: a great beauty named Estrildis, a noblewoman of Teutonic birth, kept for ransom by Humber.

As soon as King Locrinus saw Estrildis he fell instantly in love with her. Her long golden hair and slender waist excited him and her sweet tender voice made him want to protect her from every evil. The king was smitten – but there was a problem: he was already betrothed to Gwendolen. Gwendolen was from the house of Cornwall, and the engagement was a political match to strengthen his throne. Gwendolen's father was a powerful man and could not be crossed. Locrinus could not have Estrildis. To take her would be to shatter his kingdom.

But Locrinus could not give up Estrildis, because he loved her very much. He had Estrildis secretly taken to Trinovantum (later rebuilt and named Caer Lud by King Lud: today we know it as London). He hid Estrildis in a cave, guarded by trusted men at arms, and claimed that she had returned to her homeland.

The marriage of King Locrinus to Princess Gwendolen was a great occasion attended by nobles from across the land. The king and his new queen toured the land, accepting tribute and homage from the people. For seven years the king deceived his queen – pretending to be a loyal husband while sneaking away to be with his lover.

The queen gave birth to a prince and they named the child Maddan. King Locrinus, in the tradition of the Celts at the time, sent the boy to live with his grandfather in Cornwall.

Around the same time, Estrildis also gave birth: to a girl. She was a fair child. Her parents gave her the name Hafren (which was the Celtic version of the Roman name 'Sabrina').

Queen Gwendolen grew sad without her son to nurture, but she could do nothing to bring him home. Then one day, a messenger from Cornwall bought news of her father's death and her heart broke in two. King Locrinus was pleased to hear the news. He had feared the old man and knew that at last he was free to do as he pleased.

Within days Estrildis and Hafren were taken from their underground hideaway and brought to the king's castle. The king banished Gwendolen to Cornwall, where she was reunited with her son – but she was not happy. Her anger turned to hatred when she learned of her husband's years of deceit. The years passed, and as Madden grew to manhood his mother taught him to hate his father. They plotted, and planned the downfall of the king.

Madden grew into a fine warrior and, when his mother said the time was right, he marched north with an army to challenge his father. The two armies met on the banks of the Stour and in the heat of battle, Madden pulled the king from his horse and ran him through with his sword.

Following the battle, Queen Gwendolen ruled in place of her dead husband. Her first command was that her men must find Estrildis and Hafren. She wanted revenge.

The king's lover and her daughter had taken refuge in Dolforwyn castle but were quickly captured by the queen's men. They were bound and dragged from the castle. People watched with shame as the two women were paraded through the streets like common criminals.

Then, the queen's revenge was completed as Estrildis and Hafren were thrown into the river to drown, but a strange thing happened. As Hafren's lungs filled with water and her body sank down into the depths, she transformed into a goddess of the river and, to this day, glides under the water, peering up from her watery home . . .

Next time you cross the Afon Hafren – the Severn – look down and think of her under the glassy, cool, transluscent waves . . .

# Dolforwyn Castle Walk

This is a pleasant country walk that begins by climbing a short distance to Dolforwyn castle and then takes you through woodland before descending to the Montgomery Canal and the Afon Hafren. Dolforwyn castle is located near the A483 four miles north-east of Newtown and ten miles south-west of Welshpool, and not far from Montgomery (*Trefaldwyn*). Follow the CADW signpost for the castle near the village of Abermule (*Abermiwl*) and drive along the lane for two thirds of a mile to a small car park where the walk begins. You join the river at a bridge that proudly boasts it is the 'Second Iron Bridge', built in 1852. The walk then continues along the canal towpath, between the river and the canal, and finally, after a short climb, returns to the car park below the castle. Parking is free but there are no facilities along the route.

**Ordnance Survey map number 136 grid reference SO 154 949**
Latitude = 52.5460, Longitude = -3.2489
Lat = 52 degrees, 32.8 minutes North
Long = 3 degrees, 14.9 minutes West

| | |
|---|---|
| Length | 4.88 km – 3.03 miles |
| Maximum height | 224.76 metres |
| Minimum height | 85.12 metres |
| Height ascended | 212.58 metres |
| Navigation | Easy |
| Difficulty | Easy |
| Estimated time | 2 hours 12 minutes |

Leave your car and walk north-east along the lane for a few steps to the track leaving on the left. Follow the track uphill through a gate. After 100 m the track turns left and you walk south-west for 180 m past a house on your right and arrive at a wooden gate. Go

*Dolforwyn castle*

through the gate and follow the path straight on for another 200 m, where you turn right along a grassy track leading up to the castle. This track was once the main street of the town that sat below the castle and was lined with timber-framed, thatched buildings.

The castle was built towards the end of the thirteenth century by Llywelyn ap Gruffudd, Prince of Gwynedd. Llywelyn was declared the 'Prince of Wales' by a convention of Welsh leaders in 1258, and was so recognised by Henry III in the Treaty of Montgomery (1267). His ambition was to build his capital here in Dolforwyn, above the central valley of his county. It was also a border fortress designed as a stronghold against the English. As you explore the ruin it becomes apparent that the castle was not built for comfort but a bastion that would be difficult to overcome. The English king, Edward I, besieged Dolforwyn castle in 1277 and captured it. Ownership of the castle and town then passed to Roger Mortimer. The town was abandoned in 1279 when Roger Mortimer started the construction of Newtown further down the valley.

Once you have explored the castle, continue north-east along the track on the north side of the ruin. As you reach the end of the castle wall, a footpath, which you take, continues straight on through the trees for 60 m to a wooden gate. Go through the gate and follow the path downhill across a field, passing gorse bushes on your right and continuing north-east for 200 m until you reach a large oak tree in the middle of the field. As you pass the oak tree turn north and walk downhill to the bottom of the field and a footbridge over a stream.

On the other side of the stream, continue straight on uphill to a metal gate leading to a lane. Turn right along the lane for 10 m and then turn right through a metal gate leading to a footpath, where you walk east, downhill, through a field to a pond at the bottom of the field. Walk through the gate and across the pond dam so that the pond is on your right. On the far side of the dam you pass through two more gates leading into a wood. Continue along the footpath as it follows the edge of the wood and takes you east into the next valley.

The footpath continues for 250 m to a gate where it turns to the south and after 60 m you go through another gate leading to a driveway. Walk down the drive to the lane where you turn right and then immediately left along a lane with a 'dead end' sign. Continue along the lane for 200 m until you reach 'The Belfry', an unusual house on your right. Leave the lane through the gate and along the footpath on your left, opposite the house. Walk 120 m down the left-hand side of the next field, aiming for a gate in the bottom left hand corner.

*The second iron bridge over the Severn*

At the bottom of the field, go through the gate, cross the road and through the gate on the far side of the road, leading into a small field. Turn left and walk 60 m across the field towards a hedge and gate. Go through the gate onto a road and turn right for a few steps. Cross the first bridge, over the canal, and turn right walking down the slope to join the canal towpath.

You are now walking on part of the Severn Way, a 210-mile long-distance walk along the river. As you join the towpath, look at the cast iron bridge over the river on your right. It bears the words 'This second iron bridge constructed in the County of Montgomery was erected in the year 1852'. (Abraham Derby III built the first, more famous, Ironbridge across the Severn at Ironbridge Gorge in 1779.) Was it here that the unfortunate Hafren was thrown into the river?

The canal was constructed to transport lime to the upper Severn Valley to improve its agricultural yield. Eventually the canal extended from Newtown to Franklin Junction on the Llangollen Canal, a distance of 33 miles. The canal was profitable until the 1914–18 war, when it started to lose money. It was abandoned in 1936 when a major leak occurred at Franklin Bridge. The canal is of historical significance and considerable restoration has been undertaken during the last fifty years.

Follow the canal towpath for 500 m until the canal turns right and passes under the road, while the footpath goes straight on. Continue along the footpath for another 100 m where the path turns right and passes under the road in a loop, and rejoin the canal on the far side. Walk a further 550 m along the towpath until you reach bridge number 149, just before the second set of lock

*Returning along the canal towpath*

gates. Go over the bridge, through the gate, and turn left along the lane for a few steps before turning right, through a gate, following the footpath sign to Castell Dolforwyn.

The footpath now goes north east for 450 m and climbs through a field towards a gate at the top, leading to a lane. Go through the gate and turn right along the lane for 700 m until you arrive back at the car park and the starting point of your walk.

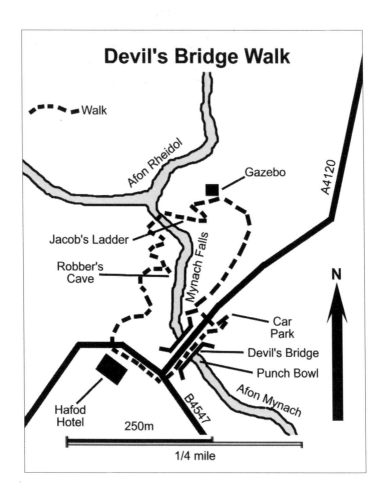

# Devil's Bridge Walk

Walk

Afon Rheidol

Gazebo

Jacob's Ladder

Mynach Falls

Robber's Cave

A4120

N

Car Park

Devil's Bridge

Punch Bowl

Hafod Hotel

B4547

Afon Mynach

250m

1/4 mile

## 9

# The Devil's Bridge

The widow, Marged, lived on the south bank of Afon Mynach. For company she kept a little dog and a cow. Each morning, as the sun's warming rays crept over the mountain, she would rise from her bed and milk her cow. The milk was rich and creamy, and Marged would make butter and cheese. Each afternoon Marged would push a heavy barrow, loaded with butter and cheese, to the village of Ponterwyd, where she would sell her produce at the crossroads. Because she could not cross the river near her house, the current being too fast, Marged had to push her simple cart along the bank of the river until it was shallow and calm enough to ford. Each evening, as the sun vanished in the west, she would trudge the long journey home along the riverbank, dragging the empty cart behind her.

'My bones ache and my legs are so stiff. If only there was a bridge; it would save me hours of walking,' she moaned, as she fell into bed.

She slept a deep troubled sleep and did not hear the rain beating on her roof, nor see the lightning flashing across the sky or hear the thunder crashing, as a great storm raged through the night.

Next morning, Marged woke and dressed. The dog, eager to start the day, scampered around her feet. She opened the door to the byre and called 'I am here, Malen' (for that was the cow's name). 'It is time to give your milk'.

Marged peered into the gloom but her precious cow was gone. The old woman ran outside. The dog followed and started to bark, excited by her confusion.

'Where are you, Malen?' cried the old woman.

Then she saw her cow. She was standing on the far bank of the river. The river was swollen with the storm, running fast and deep with a deafening roar.

Next to the cow stood a man, dressed in a monk's habit. A hood covered his head.

'Is this your cow?' yelled the monk. His voice was strangely powerful and carried easily above the thunder of the river.

The old woman replied, but her answer was carried away, drowned by the noise of the water. She nodded a reply.

'She must have been frightened and got lost in the night. You will have to walk miles upstream if you want to cross the river to collect her,' boomed the monk across the gorge.

'Oh dear! If only there was a bridge I could skip across the river and milk her in a moment,' wailed the old woman.

'Marged, I shall build you a bridge before noon,' cried the monk.

'A bridge before noon? That would be a miracle but how could I repay such a kindness? I have no money,' called the old woman.

The monk laughed. 'Money means nothing to me. All I ask in return is the soul of the first living thing that walks over the bridge,' he cried.

Marged wanted the bridge and eagerly agreed to the contract.

'Go inside your house and wait. I will call you when the bridge is finished,' yelled the monk.

Marged took her dog into the house and closed the door. Outside, a great commotion started. She could hear rocks being hammered and split, trees being felled and sawn into planks, chains clanking with heavy loads and great shouts as the monk toiled to build the bridge.

As time passed Marged grew hungry. She took some bread and cheese from the cupboard and started to eat. The noise outside stopped.

'It is ready,' called the monk.

Marged opened the door and ran outside, still holding her breakfast in her hand. The monk and her cow were standing on the far side of the river. In front of them a fine bridge with a stone arch stretched across the ravine.

'Come across and inspect your new bridge,' invited the monk.

Just as she was about to walk onto the bridge, the old woman remembered what the monk wanted in payment for his work – the soul of the first living thing that walks over the bridge. She stopped.

'Your cow needs milking. You must come and get her,' implored the monk with a devious grin.

'How can I be sure the bridge will take my weight?' called Marged.

'Come, Marged. You can see how strong the bridge is,' coaxed the monk.

'The river runs fast. I might fall in and drown,' yelled the old woman.

'Trust me. You will be quite safe,' replied the monk.

But Marged did not trust the monk.

'Here, boy,' called the old woman.

As the dog sprang up, Marged threw her bread and cheese right over the river. It landed by the monk's feet. The hungry dog chased across the bridge to the food and wolfed it down – and the first living soul had crossed the bridge!

The monk flew into a rage. His face grew red and his hood fell to his shoulders revealing two black horns. Marged had dealt with the Devil.

'I'm an old woman but I'm not an old fool. Our deal is done. Be on your way, Satan, and take your dog's soul with you,' cried Marged.

'The soul of a dog is no use to me. Keep it. You have tricked me, Marged. I won't forget this,' boomed the Devil and vanished. The old woman lived with her dog and cow for many years and people travelled from far and wide to see her fine bridge over Afon Mynach. The Devil never returned, but the bridge he built in one morning stands to this day.

*Devil's Bridge, showing the three different bridges spanning the gorge*

# Devil's Bridge Walk

The walk at Devil's Bridge (*Pontarfynach*) is the shortest in the series and unusual because it is on private land where the owners make a small charge for entry. Devil's Bridge is ten miles east of Aberystwyth on the A4120, and is at the end of the Vale of Rheidol narrow gauge railway and a major tourist attraction. It can get busy in the summer with holidaymakers arriving at Devil's Bridge on the steam trains from Aberystwyth.. There is a free car park by the bridges and public toilets in the village of Pontarfynach, opposite the railway station. There is a well-stocked shop and Post Office a little further on.

The walk begins at the three bridges over Afon Mynach and takes you down into an enchanting wooded valley with spectacular views of Mynach Falls. Payment is either by a coin operated turnstile or a manned kiosk during holiday seasons. You will need some pound coins for the turnstile. Despite the charge, the walk is worthwhile. At the bottom of the valley you cross the river and climb up the opposite side of the valley passing the 'Robber's Cave' and emerge through a second turnstile in front of the Hafod Hotel. The route is easy to follow, but while I have marked it as moderate, there are several steep runs of steps, which can be slippery when wet and might be difficult for anyone with a dodgy hip or knee. A section known as 'Jacob's Ladder' is considered to be particularly dangerous. There are handrails but, as we found during our visit, some of them are not secure and cannot be trusted.

Go through the turnstile and walk down the short flight of steps. Turn left at the bottom to a viewing area where you will see the bridges over the Mynach. There are three bridges. The first, a stone arch, which according to the legend was built by the devil,

***Ordnance Survey map number 135 grid reference SN 742 770***
Latitude = 52.3772, Longitude = -3.8492
Lat = 52 degrees, 22.6 minutes North
Long = 3 degrees, 51.0 minutes West

| | |
|---|---|
| Length | 1.08 km – 0.67 miles |
| Maximum height | 206.20m |
| Minimum height | 110.26m |
| Height ascended | 116.30m |
| Navigation | Easy |
| Difficulty | Moderate |
| Estimated time | 45 minutes |

was constructed between 1075 and 1200. A second, larger, stone bridge was built above the first in 1753. Finally, an iron bridge was added, above the second stone bridge, in 1901.

From the first viewing point walk north-east, back, past the entrance. The path takes you through woodland filled with rhododendrons, where picnic tables and bench seats have been placed so you can rest and enjoy the views. After 200 m, the path turns south and descends past the next viewing point. From here the path gets steeper and then turns east, until you arrive at a gazebo with spectacular views of the waterfalls where the Mynach falls 90 metres (300 feet) to the bottom of the gorge before it joins the Rheidol.

Continue downhill, past the gazebo, walking north-west. From here you can see the Rheidol below you on your right. After a short distance the path zigzags around a rock and then descends steeply to the valley bottom. This section is 'Jacob's Ladder'. There are handrails on both sides and barrier rails partially across the steps at regular intervals.

At the bottom the path turns and takes you over a cast iron

*Jacob's Ladder: the steps are slippery and the handrail doubtful*

arched footbridge that spans the Mynach. Below you the river rushes through a narrow channel cut in the rock and joins the Rheidol. From here you climb, with the waterfall on your left, passing viewing points as you go. One of these contains a sign indicating that you are in all that remains of the 'Robber's Cave'. According to the story, related on a plaque in the cave, two brothers, helped by their sister, used the cave as a hideout centuries ago. Following a botched robbery, when the victim was killed, they were tracked and caught, using dogs to find their lair.

The brothers were hanged at Rhaeadr, and the sister was burnt at the stake as a warning to others.

As you approach the top of the climb, there is a viewing point from where you can look back along the valley and enjoy impressive views of the Rheidol. From here you emerge through the turnstile back onto the road where you turn left past the Hafod Arms Hotel.

Just beyond the hotel there is an old Automobile Association telephone box, once used by motorists to summon help. The box would have been locked but all members had a key. AA patrolmen were instructed to salute members as they passed, except when the police were operating a speed trap in the area, when the sight of the patrolman standing to attention by his motorbike, without saluting, was intended as a warning of the policemen's trap ahead.

The road returns you over the bridge and back to the car park. As you cross the Mynach look down at the river on your right where you will see the water vanishing into a hole. This is the 'Punch Bowl', where the water has cut its way down through the rock. There is a second shorter walk, reached through a different turnstile that goes down to the river on the south side of the road. If you want a clearer view of the three bridges you will need to visit the walk to the Punch Bowl on the south side of the road.

*Just one part of the waterfall below the bridge*

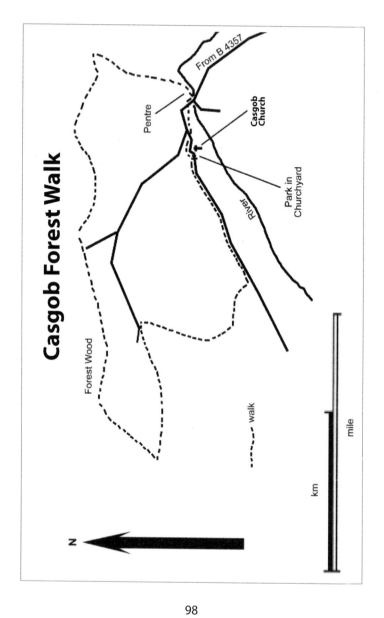

# Casgob Forest Walk

Forest Wood

Pentre

From B 4357

Casgob Church

Park in Churchyard

River

- - - walk

N

km

mile

# 10

# *Y Ddraig Goch* – The Red Dragon

The Mabinogion, an ancient book of Welsh legends, tells of the time when strange beasts walked the earth and a red dragon lived high in the Cambrian Mountains. It harmed no one and was respected by the people. The land of Wales was at peace, and when Prince Lud inherited the throne he was content to share his kingdom with the great beast. The kingdom prospered and grew larger than it is today, covering most of Britain. Lud built a new city called 'Caer Lud', later to be known as London.

But an evil tribe of dwarfs, the Coraniaid, lived in the east. The Coraniaid had ears that were so sensitive they could hear any sound whispered in the wind. They heard their neighbours in the west talking about their good fortune and grew jealous. The Coraniad invaded Lud's land armed with three weapons.

The first of these was their hearing. Because the Coraniaid could hear every word ever spoken it was impossible to plot their downfall. The Coraniaid knew everything the Welsh planned, and were ready for everything the desperate defenders tried.

The second weapon was a fearsome white dragon, which breathed fire and scorched everything in its path. The red dragon, woken from his peaceful dreams, rose up and the two mighty beasts became locked in a fearsome battle. They flew into the air, spitting plumes of fire. They clawed at each other with sharpened talons, ripping flesh, and their tails flailed the ground as they locked in combat. The screams of the battling dragons caused animals to drop dead with fear. The battle between the giant beasts continued for years as they thundered back and forth across the land. Fertile land trampled by the powerful dragons turned to barren rock. Plants withered and blew away.

The third weapon the invaders brought with them was a wicked magician who, each night, plundered the grain from storehouses of the kingdom. Every night, guards would lock themselves in the storehouses but always fell asleep, victims of the magician's spells. Each morning when they awoke the grain was gone. With no grain there was no flour and the bakers could bake no bread. With no bread to eat, the people began to starve, but still the Coraniaid advanced and the dragons battled. Lud left his kingdom and travelled to France where his wise brother, Llefelys, was king.

'Tell me, brother. What can I do to stop the Coraniaid? I fear my kingdom is lost,' he cried.

The two kings talked quietly together, speaking through a brass horn to hide their words from the Coraniaid.

'I hear tell there is a poisonous oil, made from boiled insects, which will not harm your people, but when sprinkled on the Coraniaid, will kill them instantly,' said Llefelys.

'But how will I catch them?' asked Lud.

'You must trick the invaders and trap them,' replied the wise brother.

'The dragons are destroying the land. What is to be done to stop their battle?' cried Lud.

'Your red dragon is a brave beast but he can never win against the evil white dragon. There is only one way to end the fight,' answered Llefelys.

'You are wise, my brother but do you know how to end the dragon's battle and stop the magician stealing our food?' asked Lud.

'Listen carefully,' whispered Llefelys.

Lud moved closer to his brother and pressed the brass tube tight against his ear ...

Lud returned to Wales with a cask of oil from his brother; the poison prepared from boiled insects. He called his nobles together for a secret council.

'We cannot win this war against the Coraniaid. We must surrender and show respect to our invaders. Send a messenger inviting them to the castle tomorrow to accept our homage,' he commanded.

But the Coraniaid did not need a messenger. They had heard his words.

The next day the people of Wales gathered to greet their new masters. The Coraniaid arrived with a fanfare of trumpets. Lud waited until all his enemies were together in the castle then gave a loud cry. It was the signal his warriors, on the ramparts, were waiting for. They showered poisoned oil over the throng below. It was harmless to the king's subject but every invader was killed instantly.

That night the king locked himself inside the castle's grain-store and hid in a large barrel of icy water. As it grew dark a terrible sleepiness came over the king but the freezing water kept him awake. His arms and legs grew numb and he shook with cold as he waited. Then, a strange light appeared in the room and Lud saw a little man busy moving sacks of corn. The man wore a strange cloak and muttered as he worked. It was the evil magician stealing more grain. The king leapt out of the barrel and seized the man.

'Don't hurt me,' snivelled the magician.

'Promise never again to steal our food or harm my people in any way and I will let you go,' cried the king.

'I honour you, great Lud. The Coraniaid tricked me and made me steal from you. You have my pledge,' promised the magician, and swore a magic oath that he would keep his word.

The invaders were gone but their ferocious white dragon was still at war, battling with the red dragon. Lud gave orders for a huge pit to be dug. The men filled the pit with mead and covered it with cloth. As the two giant beasts fought they fell into the pit and, thirsty from the years of fighting, drank their fill of mead. Both dragons fell into a drunken sleep. The king's men tied them both with stout ropes and buried them in a stone vault deep beneath the mountain Dinas Emrys in Snowdonia where, according to the Mabinogion, they remain until this day.

The king, however, was proud of the red dragon of Wales that had fought so valiantly and for so long to protect his kingdom. He had the red dragon secretly removed from the vault and taken to the dark forest of Radnor, a lonely place, where it could sleep and recover from its wounds. To protect the dragon from evil, the king ordered that four churches be built surrounding the forest. The Churches of Llanfihangel Cefnllys, Llanfihangel Rhydiddon, Llanfihangel Nant Melan and Llanfihangel Cascob were all dedicated to St Michael and, it is said, if any of the churches are ever destroyed, the red dragon of Wales will wake and rise up from its secret hiding place, ready to do battle once more.

# Casgob Forest Walk

Radnor Forest is a large area of remote countryside with army firing ranges to the west. This is a walk where you will meet few other ramblers. The sleepy village of Casgob is the location of St Michael's church, one of the four churches built to protect the sleeping red dragon. Casgob is at the eastern end of the forest. Our walk starts from the church and climbs up the lane to Twiscob and then takes you higher along a bridleway over the mountain with stunning views in all directions. The walk then continues in a circular route through Forest Wood and descends, returning you to Casgob, passing Pentre Farm as you go. It's only when you see the vastness of the forest that you can really appreciate why Lud chose this remote place to hide the Red Dragon.

Casgob is located at the end of a 2-mile single track lane which begins on the B4357, 2.7 miles east of Presteigne (*Llanandras*) and 4 miles south of Knighton (*Trefyclo*). There are no toilet facilities on this walk and parking is limited in the village but it is possible to park in the back of the churchyard – although care needs to be taken not to let the resident sheep (who cut the grass) escape as you drive through the gate.

Casgob church was built in the thirteenth century and restored in 1895. It is normally locked but a key is available from the cottage opposite. In the porch is a sign telling you that in 1878 new pews were installed for £25 and, according to the terms on which they were installed, they are free for parishioners to use. In the seventeenth century the church was used for an exorcism when Elizabeth Lloyd was possessed by demons. In the north wall of the nave there is a plaque with zodiac signs and the incantation used.

**Ordnance Survey map number 137 grid reference SO 238 664**
Latitude = 52.2906, Longitude = -3.1177
Lat = 52 degrees, 17.4 minutes North
Long = 3 degrees, 7.1 minutes West

| | |
|---|---|
| Length | 6.77 km – 4.20 miles. |
| Maximum height | 405.96 m |
| Minimum height | 224.11 m |
| Height ascended | 251.58 m |
| Navigation | Easy |
| Difficulty | Moderate |
| Estimated time | 2 hour 55 minutes |

Leave the church and walk west along the lane. After a short distance, the lane bears south-west and you climb at a steady rate for 1.1 km until you reach the top with a bridle path on your right. Turn right and follow the bridle path up through a yard to a metal gate. Go through the gate and continue straight on up the hill. You now have a steep climb for 500 m along a wide grassy bridle path. At the top there are superb views towards Ludlow and Leominster in the east, Beacon Hill to the north, and the Forest of Radnor to the west. If the army is on manoeuvres you may hear the artillery fire from the ranges at Harley Dingle on the other side of the forest.

Turn right at the top of your climb and walk north, through a wooden gate, so that you follow the track with a wood on your right. After a short distance you go through a second gate and continue downhill along the track. After 500 m you will arrive at a T-junction where you turn left. Walk along the track for 80 m until you reach two metal gates. Go through the left-hand gate following the sign with a blue arrow on a yellow circle.

This leads into a field, where you continue west following the

*St Michael's church, Casgob, one of the churches
built to surround the Red Dragon*

right-hand fence line. After 220 m you go through another gate
into the next field and continue in the same direction for 155 m.
This brings you to a gate leading to a third field which you cross,
again keeping to the right-hand side. Aim for a gate 400 m away
in the far right hand corner of the field.

Go through the gate and turn right along the forestry track.
This will take you downhill into Forest Wood. Walk along the track
in a north-easterly direction for 500 m until you reach a junction.
Bear right at the junction and continue uphill through the wood
for 300 m to the next junction where you bear left and walk east.

After 600 m, go straight over a crossroads and walk on a
further 100 m where you turn right and start to climb once more.
This track starts by taking you south-east and then turns east,
giving you good views of Casgob in the valley on your right.

Follow the track to its end, a distance of 850 m. At the end of the track, go straight on along the footpath, marked with a blue arrow on a yellow circle.

Follow the footpath for 110 m to a gate leading onto open heath populated with bracken and gorse. The footpath now turns to the left and descends over bare rock before it turns to the right and emerges at a junction of footpaths and bridleways with a stone bluff on your left.

*Looking north from Forest Wood*

Turn sharp left and descend south along the bridle path. The bridle path continues downhill for 700 m, emerging at Pentre Farm and a road junction. Turn right along the road for 70 m until you reach a footpath sign and a gate on your left. Go through the gate and walk west across the field aiming for the larger metal gate in the far corner of the field. This will bring you back to the road where you turn right and walk the short distance back to the churchyard.

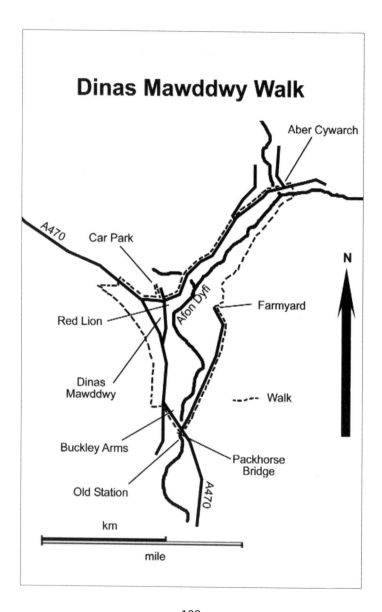

# Dinas Mawddwy Walk

Aber Cywarch

A470

Car Park

Red Lion

Afon Dyfi

Farmyard

Dinas
Mawddwy

- - - Walk

N

Buckley Arms

Packhorse
Bridge

Old Station

A470

km

mile

# 11

# The Red Bandits of Mawddwy

In the sixteenth century the land of Meirionnydd was a wild and dangerous place. Gangs of robbers roamed the countryside. They terrorized the people; stealing, cheating and murdering at will. The most treacherous were the Red Bandits of Mawddwy, a gang so evil that villagers shook in fear when they swaggered past. The bandits had bright red hair, which they wore long as a mark of allegiance to their clan.

Fearing for their safety, villagers never left home without weapons. At night, doors were locked, windows shuttered and barred. Some put sharpened scythes in their chimneys to stop the robbers entering down the flue and murdering them in their beds.

The Red Bandits of Mawddwy spoke a strange language that only they understood. People whispered that they had arrived from a distant land in the east, exiled for their evil ways.

News of the Red Bandits of Mawddwy reached Queen Mary. She summoned the Sheriff of Meirionnydd, Baron Lewis Owen, and commanded him to end the reign of terror of the Red Bandits. Baron Owen gathered together his men and attacked the bandits while they slept in their hideout on Dinas Mawddwy. Many bandits were slain in the fight and those that survived were led away in chains.

Baron Owen ordered a gallows to be built. Eighty men were separated from the women and led to the scaffold.

'I will end your tyranny,' shouted the baron. 'Hang all the men,' he ordered.

One by one the bandits were placed on the scaffold and dropped with a sickening jolt as the noose snapped their necks. The women screamed and pleaded for mercy but the baron ignored their cries. Among the condemned men were two young boys. Their mother, Lowri, broke away from the other women. She fell on her knees in front of the baron and grabbed his coat.

'My Lord! They are just boys,' she wailed. 'Please be merciful: spare their lives,' she sobbed.

The baron looked down at the prostrate woman. He lifted his boot and kicked her to the ground.

'Hang the two boys next,' he commanded.

When it was done, Lowri stood up, a sullen look of hatred in her eyes. She bared her chest and cupped her breasts with her hands.

'These yellow breasts have given suck to life and these hands will be washed in your blood,' she spat.

The baron snorted at the demented woman and strode away leaving her standing by the bodies of her two children.

The tyranny of the Red Bandits of Mawddwy was broken – but the red-haired women wanted revenge for the murder of their menfolk. They waited and plotted, until one day the Baron was out riding with his retainers. Suddenly, as they trotted through the valley at Bwlch Oerddrws, a hail of arrows rained down on the riders. The riders were unable to protect themselves and were cut down. More arrows followed. The baron's horse, wounded with an arrow through its neck, fell to the ground.

The baron was alone; all his men were dead or wounded. Red-haired women emerged from behind rocks. They seized the baron and bound him with leather thongs. The prisoner was dragged to a camp hidden high in the forest above Dinas Mawddwy.

A woman emerged from a cave. It was Lowri, the mother of the two boys. Her face was contorted with hate. With her was an old man with red hair.

'Strip the baron and tie him to that tree,' commanded the woman.

The baron struggled as hands ripped his cloak and tunic from his shoulders. His arms were pulled back and lashed to a stout tree.

'What evil is this?' he cried.

The man produced a knife and walked towards the baron. Lowri stood in front of the baron.

She cupped her hands.

The baron screamed as the old man raised the knife. Then, with one quick movement, he slashed the baron's throat. The baron looked down, silently, and watched while the vengeful woman washed her hands in the blood spurting from the wound in his neck. Then he died.

Baron Lewis Owen, Sheriff of Meirionnydd, was murdered on 12 October 1555. The old man known as John Goch (*goch* = red), a relative of the young boys, was captured and charged with striking the lethal blow. His accomplice, Lowri, was tried at Bala in 1558. She claimed to be a spinster and attempted to avoid the gallows by announcing that she was pregnant. A jury of women confirmed the pregnancy and she was not hanged while carrying the child. No record exists to confirm whether or not she was executed after giving birth.

# Dinas Mawddwy Walk

Remote mountain roads and its position on an important route across Wales made Dinas Mawddwy a perfect base for bandits. Today, the same magnificent scenery surrounding the Llaethnant valley makes the area ideal walking country. The walk starts from the centre of the village and heads north-east to the hamlet of Aber Cywarch, where it crosses the river. From here the route turns south-west across farmland and then climbs north following the forestry tracks around Foel Dinas before finally returning to Dinas Mawddwy. The village is located on the A470, nine miles east of Dolgellau and eleven miles north-east of Machynlleth. There is a free car park and toilets on Dyfi Terrace, opposite the Red Lion public house.

*Ordnance Survey map number 125 grid reference SH 858 149*
Latitude = 52.7203, Longitude = -3.6916
Lat = 52 degrees, 43.2 minutes North
Long = 3 degrees, 41.5 minutes West

| | |
|---|---|
| Length | 6.08 km – 3.78 miles |
| Maximum height | 223.49 m |
| Minimum height | 73.32 m |
| Height ascended | 277.79 m |
| Navigation | Easy |
| Difficulty | Moderate |
| Estimated time | 2 hours 47 minutes |

Walk south to the end of Dyfi Terrace and turn left along the road so that the Red Lion is on your right. This is, apparently, the oldest building in the village, but it was not the pub used by the robbers. They drank at another hostelry, now named the Brigands Inn, which is south of the village.

*The old packhorse bridge over the Dyfi*

Follow the road as it takes you north-east out of the village. The mountain on your left is Foel Benddin, which rises to 543 m (1700 ft) and the river below you, on the right, is the Dyfi. After 930 m the road forks and you bear right continuing for another 530 m into Aber Cywarch. When you reach the hamlet the road crosses the Cywarch, a tributary of the Dyfi. 70 m further on you reach a gate on the right leading down to a footbridge over the Dyfi.

Go through the gate, over the footbridge, into the field, and turn right following the path along the bank of the river. Continue for 500 m to a stile leading into a wood. Cross the stile and follow the path through the wood for 180 m to another stile, where you go straight on. A further 170 m brings you to a gate where the path climbs away from the river and, after 140 m, emerges at a gate leading into a field. Go through the gate and walk south-west for 50 m to a gate leading to the next field.

The path goes across the field still heading south-west and aiming for the bottom left-hand corner where, after 320 m, you arrive at a gate leading to a track. Go through the gate and follow the track for a short distance until you reach a gate on the right leading to a small field and another gate, which is the rear entrance to the farmyard. Cross the farmyard and turn left along a lane so that you are walking south through the valley. Walk along the lane for 730 m until you arrive at a gate leading to a caravan park. Go through the gate and walk along the lane through the caravan park, so that you emerge onto the road outside.

On the opposite side of the road you can see two arches of a packhorse bridge built over 300 years ago. Beyond the bridge is the entrance to what was a railway station. In 1856 a Manchester businessman bought the manor of Mawddwy as a present for his son. The son, Edward Buckley, decided that he wanted a train set and started to build one. The railway was opened in 1867 when the young Mr. Buckley rode triumphantly on the engine along the seven-mile line. The line carried passengers until 1931 and continued with freight, mainly slate from a quarry further up the mountain, until it closed in 1950. The house just inside the gates was the station building and the platform still exists. The old engine sheds have since been converted to a mill and woollen shop catering for tourists.

Edward Buckley built a new manor house for himself, cottages for his workers, a chapel for worshippers and a hotel for visitors, opposite the station. The Buckley Arms Hotel was built using reinforced concrete, a building material that had recently been invented. Mr Buckley was made a baronet in 1868 and set about spending his father's fortune with increasing enthusiasm. He

*Terminus of Dinas Mawddwy railway line.*
*The station is now a private house*

opened quarries, lead and copper mines, cut a new road around the mountain to bypass Dinas Mawddwy and was a major investor, as well as founding Director, of 'The Channel Tunnel Company'. On 19 May 1876 he filed for bankruptcy. Even as his assets were being seized and sold he was completing a grand new Regency-style house for himself in Worthing. His father's wealth had all gone. Buckley continued to live in Dinas Mawddwy after his debts were settled but became a recluse. He died in 1910.

Leave the station and walk north west along the main road for 200 m, passing the Buckley Arms on your right. Turn left in front of the war memorial and then immediately right, along Godre'd Coed, passing two modern houses clad with slate, on your left. Turn right along the forestry track just behind houses and walk north. The track climbs steadily as it takes you 1 km around Foel

Dinas. As you proceed, you pass a disused quarry on your left with walls that are covered with rhododendron plants, like a giant hanging garden. The floor of the quarry is now the site of a water treatment plant. Look east and you will enjoy fantastic views across the valley you walked through earlier.

240 m beyond the quarry leave the track and turn right, following a footpath sign pointing down some steps. The narrow footpath descends east for 200 m where it turns and emerges at the main road. Turn right, walk 160 m along the road and then turn left down the road to Dinas Mawddwy and Dyfi Terrace, which will be on the left.

*The Brigands Arms, where, it is said,*
*the bandits would drink and wait for their victims*

*Follow the lane towards the hamlet of Aber Cywarch*

*The valley is full of interesting buildings*

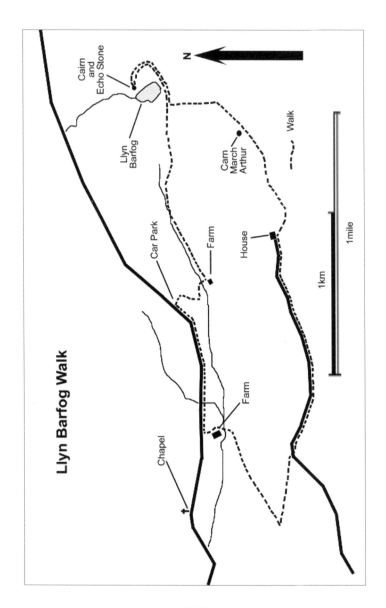

Llyn Barfog Walk

Cairn and Echo Stone

Llyn Barfog

Carn March Arthur

Car Park

Farm

House

Farm

Chapel

N

Walk

1km

1mile

## 12

# The Beast of Llyn Barfog

There was a time when strange animals roamed the land and people stayed home, near a blazing fire, after dark. No one ventured near Llyn Barfog, for here lived the Afanc, a dreadful monster loathed by all. The Afanc spent its days hidden deep in the weeds and slime. At night it came out to hunt and fill its belly: a creature half crocodile, half beaver, with teeth like razors and a scaly hide like armour. It stalked the land devouring animals and anyone foolish enough to be out when the sky was black.

Sometimes the Afanc would surprise its prey and eat it in one gulp. Sometimes it would stun its victim with a slow poison that left the mind alert while paralysing the body. Late in the night, a dog would howl or a man would scream as he was slowly dragged down into the lake, to be eaten later. Widows would find the bones of their husbands on the shore of the lake, gnawed and white.

Young Arthur heard of the dreadful beast that was terrorising the land and resolved to kill it. He talked to his friend Merlin.

'How can I kill such an animal, Merlin?' he asked.

'To kill the Afanc, first you have to catch it but beware of its poison,' answered Merlin.

Arthur went to the blacksmith.

'Heat your forge, blacksmith. Build me a chain strong enough and long enough to catch the Afanc,' he cried.

The blacksmith forged links from the finest iron. He added

carbon for strength, hammering it into the red hot metal. Link by link, the chain was made until it was long enough to catch the Afanc.

Arthur's strongest battlehorse, Llamrai, was saddled. The great iron chain was loaded onto twenty carts and oxen slowly pulled the heavy loads to the lake. All was quiet. The monster was asleep somewhere in the murky depths below.

Men at arms spread the chain around the lake, surrounding the tranquil water. Arthur, resplendent in shining armour, mounted Llamrai. The ends of the chain were harnessed to the noble beast.

'Come, friend. There is work to be done,' cried Arthur.

The great warhorse walked forward. The chains pulled tight. Llamrai leaned forward into the traces, using all his strength. Slowly, the stallion began to draw the heavy chains into the water, and then they stopped. Llamrai strained and pulled with all his might but the chains would not move.

'We are stuck,' cried Arthur.

Then, the surface of the lake erupted and the Afanc burst up into the air. Its tail thrashed the water and its body writhed.

'The chain – it's wrapped around the monster's leg!' yelled Arthur.

The Afanc submerged once more and began to pull Arthur and his steed back, towards the lake.

'Hold fast, Llamrai!' cried Arthur.

Hearing his master's command, Llamrai stretched every sinew as never before. The Afanc rolled and twisted as it tried to break free. It gnawed the chain with its razor-sharp teeth but the carbon did its work and the links did not fail. The battle raged for hours with no sign of ending. As he strained, the great horse stamped the ground. Its hooves cut deep into the rock.

Then without warning, the Afanc charged at speed, out of the water, straight towards Arthur and his mount. Llamrai was taken by surprise and stumbled forward. Arthur was thrown to the ground. Quickly, he sprang up and drew his sword. The Afanc advanced towards him, spitting vile poison as he came. Arthur covered his eyes to protect them from the poisonous spray. He lifted his sword and plunged it into the neck of the attacking monster with as much force as he could muster, killing it instantly. And so ended the reign of terror of the Afanc.

The marks where Llamrai's hooves cut into the rock can still be seen near the shore of Llyn Barfog today.

# Llyn Barfog Walk

This walk starts in Cwm Maethlon. Victorian visitors – renowned for interfering with place-names – called the Cwm 'Happy Valley', and when you see the valley it is easy to understand why; it is an enchanting and almost secret place. The walk climbs east to the lake where you visit the Echo Stone and then turns south, walking past Carn March Arthur and along a path with spectacular views across the Dyfi. You then walk west with views across Cwm Maethlon before descending and returning to the car park along a quiet country lane. Llyn Barfog is in the Snowdonia National Park (*Parc Cenedlaethol Eryri*) just north of the Dyfi Estuary and the town of Aberdyfi, which is 10 miles north of Aberystwyth. To reach the start of the walk travel east from Aberdyfi along the A493, and take a turning on your left, 4 miles from the town, signposted to Cwm Maethlon. Follow the small country lane for 3.2 miles to a National Trust free car park which is on your left. This is a remote walk with no toilets or other facilities.

*Ordnance Survey map number 135 grid reference SN 640 986*
Latitude = 52.5683, Longitude = -4.0079
Lat = 52 degrees, 34.1 minutes North
Long = 4 degrees, 0.5 minutes West

| | |
|---|---|
| Length | 7.27 km – 4.51 miles |
| Maximum height | 250.14 m |
| Minimum height | 58.00 m |
| Height ascended | 296.12 m |
| Navigation | Easy |
| Difficulty | Moderate |
| Estimated time | 3 hours 13 minutes |

Leave the car park and walk south-east downhill along the track below the car park. When you reach a bungalow on your left,

*Looking east from Llyn Barfog. The walk begins in the valley below*

continue through the gate, which is across the track. The track takes you downhill and turns to the right passing farm buildings on your right. Immediately after the farm buildings the track turns to the left, passes over a stream and into a farmyard.

Fairies, according to folklore, once farmed in Cwm Maethlon, and the valley was full of contented animals. One story relates the tale of a greedy farmer who took a cow from the fairies. The cow produced fine calves and the farmer grew rich but when the cow grew old and the farmer decided to send it for slaughter, his luck changed for the worse. A fairy woman arrived at his farm. She called the cow and her calves away and they all vanished into Llyn Barfog, leaving the farmer destitute.

Turn left in the farmyard and walk uphill along the track heading east. The track continues through a dry stone wall with a ladder stile and gate and climbs with the stream on your left. Keep

123

following the track up the valley. After 200 m you go through another stone wall with a gate and stile where the track continues straight on. When you reach a footpath sign suggesting that you leave the track on the right, ignore it and continue uphill along the track. 610 m beyond the last stile you will arrive at another stone wall with gate and stile across the track. Continue climbing along the track for another 160 m, until you can see a wire fence with a metal gate at the top of the rise and to the right of the track. Leave the track and walk towards the gate.

As you reach the gate, the lake will come into view. Continue east for 200 m, following the path beyond the gate to a junction and a path leaving to the right. The path on the right is the route by which you will begin the return section of the walk and it is worth noting where it is. Continue east so that the lake is on your left. Go through a small gate and walk straight on for 270 m until you reach a slate post engraved with a hand pointing north and the words 'To Echo'. Follow the path north and then north-west for 160 m to a cairn on the north-east side of the lake. Our efforts of yelling to produce an echo were a failure, but you may have better success.

Return the way you came, back to the junction in the footpath on the south-west side of the lake where you turn left and walk south. Initially the path climbs and then enters the next valley where, after 300 m, you join a track and walk south-west through a gate. Keep walking along the track for 250 m where you will find a small cairn marked with a slate post on the right hand side of the track. This is 'Carn March Arthur' and if you look closely you will see the imprints of hoof prints cut deep into the rock; evidence, it is said, of the great battle between Arthur and the Afanc.

The track continues south-west for 610 m and gives spectacular long-distance views over the Dyfi Estuary, with Borth and Cardigan Bay stretching away to the south. The track now

*Llyn Barfog on a frosty January morning:*
*the 'Echo' is the cairn to the right of the lake*

turns right and after 140m brings you to a remote house. Go through the two metal gates on the left of the house and walk west along the tarmac lane. Below you on your right is Cwm Maethlon. Copper and lead mines operated in the valley below the house during the eighteenth century but became unprofitable and eventually closed.

After 120 m the lane goes through a metal gate and continues west for 680 m to another gate. This section of the walk gives good views of Cwm Maethlon with farmhouses dotted along the valley floor. At one time, residents of Aberdyfi were buried in Cwm Maethlon and the coffins were carried over the mountain on horse-drawn biers. If you look north-west there is a small chapel in the valley where they were laid to rest.

Continue past the gate for 540 m where you leave the lane

following a track to the right so that you are walking west and downhill into the valley. After 100 m you go through a gate and continue straight on for 340 m. The track now turns right so that you are walking north-east and continuing to descend into the valley. Follow the track for 460 m to a gate leading into a conifer wood where you go straight on through the wood for 250 m to the next gate.

The track now emerges from the wood and after 90 m arrives at a stream with a ford and a small footbridge, leading to farm buildings. Cross the stream and walk north keeping the buildings on your left, until after 130 m you reach a junction with a lane where you turn right.

The last part of the walk is an easy 1 km stroll along the lane following the valley bottom back to the car park.

*Looking west from Llyn Barfog*

*Follow the path towards the lake*

*Llyn Barfog seen from the Echo Stone*

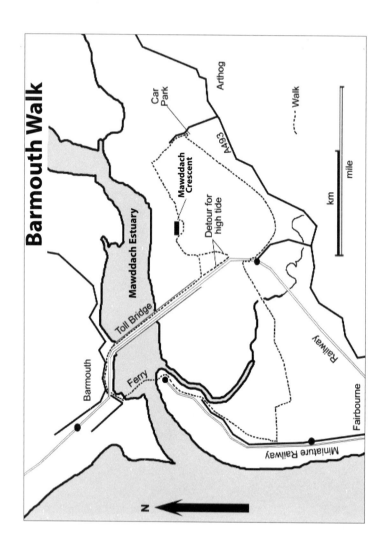

# Barmouth Walk

Arthog

Car Park

A493

Mawddach Crescent

Detour for high tide

Mawddach Estuary

Toll Bridge

Barmouth

Ferry

Railway

Fairbourne

Miniature Railway

--- Walk

km    mile

N

# 13

# The Salt Smugglers of Mawddach

In 1693, King William III was short of cash. 'I need more money,' he told his tax collectors.

'Tea, Bibles, brandy, wine, lace, candles, linen: we are taxing everything we can think of,' they replied.

'That's not good enough,' shouted the king.

'What about a tax on windows?' said one of the tax collectors.

'That's a silly idea,' answered the king.

'I know, a tax on salt,' suggested another.

'Salt!' sneered the king.

'Your majesty, everyone in the kingdom uses salt for cooking. They must have salt to preserve fish and meat. Bakers use salt to make bread, and dairies need salt to make butter,' they explained.

'A salt tax will make your majesty lots of money,' added the tax collectors.

'It's a capital idea. I like it,' replied the king.

Salt offices were set up throughout the land and the tax collectors began their unpopular work. King William was pleased – but he was an extravagant monarch. 'I need more money,' he cried.

'There are still the windows. We haven't taxed them yet,' said his tax collectors.

'I agree. We will have a tax on windows,' ordered the king.

The revenue men built Custom Houses across the land to collect the tax. One was built at Barmouth, at the mouth of the Afon Mawddach.

Sir William Jones lived in a grand house near the town. Each day the people saw him out riding a beautiful horse or being driven in his carriage. 'What a refined gentleman. He must come from a noble family,' they said as he rode past.

But Sir William had a dark secret: he was the leader of a ruthless gang of smugglers. When the nights were dark, his men would quietly row down the Afon Mawddach, past the harbour entrance and out to sea, where ships would anchor, waiting for the smugglers and the morning tide.

'What's the cargo?' whispered Sir William to a ship's captain on such a night.

'1000 bushels of salt from Ireland,' replied the captain.

'It will be a good pay day for the revenue men when you land at Barmouth,' smirked Sir William.

'Aye, it's a crime. The tax is more than the salt is worth,' replied the captain.

'I can take 500 bushels and pay you gold,' said Sir William and shook his purse to show he had the coins.

The crew unloaded the sacks of salt into the little boats while Sir William went with the captain to his cabin and paid his debt.

'Let us toast our good fortune,' said the captain and poured two glasses of brandy.

'To the king. Thanks for his greed, the people's hatred, and our good luck,' said Sir William and took a gulp. He drained the glass. 'It's a fine brandy. Do you have any more?' he asked.

'Aye, twenty barrels hidden in the hold,' replied the captain.

'I'll buy them all,' cried Sir William.

They agreed a price and the barrels of brandy were loaded into the boats. 'Look out for the revenue cutter,' called the captain as the smugglers began to row away.

Sir William smiled to himself. He knew exactly where the revenue men were. He had paid them well to stay in their beds. The smugglers were safely ashore before the sun came up.

'Where shall we hide the contraband?' asked One-eyed Jack.

'Use the cave at Trwyn Glanmor,' answered Sir William.

One-eyed Jack was a surly fellow and as greedy as his master. He took four barrels of brandy for himself and hid them in Llanaber churchyard. The hollow table-tomb in the graveyard was his own secret hiding place.

Sir William soon discovered the theft but he said nothing about it.

'We have heavy work to do tonight,' said Sir William a few nights later.

The tide carried the little boats quickly out to sea where a ship was waiting. 'We must be quick about our work tonight. There is a new revenue officer in Barmouth who can't be bribed,' whispered Sir William.

The men worked quietly while their leader paid the ship's master.

'Where are you bound?' asked Sir William.

'We sail for America,' replied the captain.

'Here is an extra 100 guineas,' said Sir William.

'What's it for?' asked the skipper.

'I want you to take One-eyed Jack with you and throw him overboard when you are far out to sea,' replied Sir William.

'That's easy money,' said the captain and took the hundred guineas. The smugglers left One-eyed Jack bound and gagged in the hold of the ship.

Years passed and Sir William forgot about One-eyed Jack. The revenue men were offering rewards for information and went armed, intent on shooting smugglers on sight. Smuggling was getting dangerous and Sir William wanted to retire. 'One last trip and that's it,' he promised himself.

The moon was in its first quarter and there was a light offshore breeze as the smugglers rowed downstream. They passed Barmouth harbour and were soon out to sea. The sea was choppy and the smugglers had to row hard.

'There she is, on the port side,' called Sir William pointing to a ship.

As they approached the ship another vessel came into view. The smugglers heard a cry, 'Heave to or we open fire.'

'It's the customs men! Row for your lives!' yelled Sir William. A cannon roared and one of the smugglers' boats disintegrated. Sir William's boat made it to the ship. He clambered aboard, leaving his men floundering below. On the deck a row of muskets were levelled at his chest.

'Move and my men will shoot you down,' said the Revenue Officer. Then, 'Is this the man?' he asked.

A man stepped out of the shadows. 'That's him. Sir William Jones, Gentleman, murderer and smuggler. Remember my reward and that you promised him to me,' said the man, pointing to Sir William. It was One-eyed Jack, who had not died, as Sir William had believed.

'You'll get your reward money. As for him; I'm as good as my word,' said the Revenue Officer and ordered his men ashore.

'What about me?' cried Sir William.

'We are going on a little sea voyage together,' sneered One-eyed Jack, and laughed.

Sir William Jones, Gentleman, from Barmouth, was never seen again.

# Barmouth Walk

This is a figure-of-eight walk that starts near the village of Arthog and goes west along a pretty, disused railway line that forms part of the Mawddach Trail and then follows the sea defences to Fairbourne (*Y Friog*). From there you turn north towards Barmouth (*Abermo*) and cross the harbour entrance using the small passenger ferry. The walk then re-crosses the Mawddach Estuary using Barmouth Bridge (a small toll is sometimes collected) before following the southern shoreline of the estuary in an easterly direction back to the starting point. The Mawddach estuary is an area of outstanding beauty and the views of the river and Cadair Idris are stunning.

*Ordnance Survey map number 124 grid reference SH 640 148*
Latitude = 52.7136, Longitude = -4.0142
Lat = 52 degrees, 42.8 minutes North
Long = 4 degrees, 0.9 minutes West

| | |
|---|---|
| Length | 9.70 km – 6.02 miles |
| Maximum height | 30.92 m |
| Minimum height | 0.00 m |
| Height ascended | 98.14 m |
| Navigation | Easy |
| Difficulty | Easy |
| Estimated time | 3 hours 20 minutes |

The passenger ferry does not run during the winter months so, if you are planning a winter excursion, you may need to modify the walk and use the toll bridge in both directions. To reach the start of the walk, head for Dolgellau and then drive west along the A493 for 5½ miles. As you pass through the village of Arthog you will see a small-gated road on your right. Go through the gate and follow the road for a quarter of a mile where you will find

'Snowdonia National Park – Arthog' car park, next to the Mawddach Trail. This is a free car park with picnic tables. There are public toilets on the Mawddach Trail and on both sides of the ferry crossing into Barmouth.

There is a small wooden gate on the north side of the car park leading to the Mawddach Trail. Go through the gate and turn left along the trail. The trail follows the old Ruabon (*Rhiwabon*) to Morfa Mawddach railway line, opened in 1865, and was used to bring holidaymakers to the popular resort town of Barmouth. Following the invention of the motor car, the line fell into decline and was closed in 1965, a time when many small railway lines were axed.

Follow the path south-west, through woodland, for 1 km where it starts to curve to the right. Continue for another 500 m until you arrive at a gate leading to a road. Go through the gate and continue along the Mawddach Trail, which is on the right of the road. After 170 m you will reach an old railway platform with public toilets and picnic tables. When the railway was operating, the track split here allowing trains to continue north, over the bridge, into Barmouth or south along the coast. At its peak this was one of the busiest railway junctions in Wales.

Continue along the trail for another 70 m to Morfa Mawddach station, which still operates. Cross the track through the gates at the end of the platform, and turn right so that you are walking north with the railway track on your right. After a short distance you turn left through a kissing gate and walk south-west along a dyke built to keep out the sea. The dyke separates farmland on your left from the mudflats and the estuary on your right.

After 320 m there is a kissing gate where the footpath zigzags between rocks, and then passes though another gate before continuing south-west for another 180 m, where the path turns

*The walk starts with a pleasant stroll along the bed
of the old railway track – part of the Mawddach Trail*

west following the line of the dyke. The popular holiday town of
Fairbourne is ahead on your left and a miniature railway chugs
along the coast between Fairbourne and Barmouth Harbour.

Keep walking west for another 850 m where the path turns
abruptly right for 180 m and then left again heading for the sea
and passing a golf course on your left. Another 350 m brings you
to a road and the miniature railway, where you turn right and walk
down the slope in front of the road. From here, the footpath goes
north-east across Ardal Hamdden recreation area signposted with
a list of things you are not allowed to do. Aim for the larger hill
behind Barmouth. This is Dinas Olau and is National Trust
property.

During the Second World War a military training camp was
established in Barmouth. In February 1944, three local schoolboys

135

*Follow the path along the dyke between the farmland and salt marshes*

broke into an armoury on the promenade and stole rifles together with a quantity of ammunition, which they took up Dinas Olau to play with. Hearing shooting and fearing a German attack, the camp commandant ordered his men to clear the hill of the enemy. The unfortunate soldiers were still searching for the attackers when the boys returned home for tea; they were never caught.

Continue north-east for 1.35 km until you reach 'Barmouth Ferry Station' and the end of the miniature railway. From here you catch the passenger ferry, a small motorboat, across the estuary to Barmouth. Turn right along the harbour wall following the road under the railway bridge, where you turn right so that you are walking east.

Just after the railway bridge you will pass a marble carving of three fishermen hauling in their nets. A local sculptor caved the marble after it was recovered from a shipwreck off the coast of

Barmouth. It is believed that the Italian marble block, one of forty-three found on the seabed, was intended for the decoration of St Paul's Cathedral. Records show the marble was shipped but never arrived at its destination.

Keep walking east along the road until you reach a path, on your right, leading down to the railway bridge. Follow the path through the tollbooth onto the bridge. As you cross the bridge there are superb views of the estuary, the harbour and the mountains.

The mountain Cadair Idris, supposedly the chair belonging to a giant named Idris, is south of the Mawddach estuary. Its highest peak, Mynydd Moel, is 2,800 feet. Bardic legend says that if you sleep on the mountain, you will wake either a poet or mad.

*The Mawddach estuary with Cadair Idris in the background*

*Crossing the estuary from Fairbourne to Barmouth*

During the eighteenth century the Mawddach Estuary was filled with shipyards. Over 100 sailing ships were launched from here between 1770 and 1827. The river would have been filled with ships from across the known world. The railway bridge, built in 1867, would have closed the river to tall sailing ships.

Cross the bridge and go through the gate at the far end. Shortly after the gate there is a stile on your left leading to a footpath along a slate bank that goes east for 220 m. If the tide is particularly high this route may be blocked. If it is, continue south-east along the main path for 330 m and then turn sharp left so that you are walking north, to return to the point at the far end of the bank. From here you follow the footpath with the estuary on your left. The path winds around a small hill called Fegla Fawr and arrives on the shore at a line of Victorian houses.

This is Mawddach Crescent and was built in 1902 by Cardiff businessman Solomon Andrews. He planned to build a luxury holiday resort in the valley but abandoned the project when the last house to be built, number 9, collapsed due to subsidence.

The footpath takes you behind Mawddach Crescent and then returns to the shore for 120 m where you turn right through a gate and then left through a second gate, following a yellow arrow on a green background. Continue east for a short distance when the path turns to the right and then bears right following the footpath sign '*Llwybr Cyhoeddus*' (= public footpath).

The path leads you away from the shore and east across scrubland for 500 m to a track. Turn right along the narrow footpath in front of the track and follow it south-east for 250 m to a lane where you turn right. Walk south-east along the lane, passing though a metal gate, and after 200 m you will arrive back at the car park.

*The railway bridge across the Mawddach, looking south*

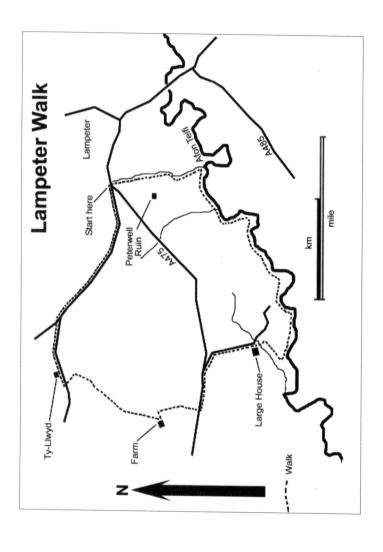

# Lampeter Walk

Lampeter

Aton Teifi

A485

Start here

Peterwell Ruin

A475

Ty-Llwyd

Farm

Large House

Walk

km

mile

N

## 14

# The Curse of Maesyfelin

Sir Francis Lloyd, owner of the Estates of Maesyfelin, was a Royalist supporter and Gentleman of the Privy Chamber to Charles II. He was Lord of Lampeter and came from an ancient and respectable lineage. Helping the king with his toilet was a task that gave Sir Francis power and prestige. His estate was large and he needed to provide an heir, but his wife was barren. The solution was simple: he took a mistress.

Bridget was twenty-five years younger than Sir Francis and their union produced two sons, Charles and Lucius. The boys were quickly named as his legal heirs in Sir Francis's will. A regular visitor to the Great House at Maesyfelin was the vicar of Llandovery. He was an old friend and advisor to Sir Francis. One day, the vicar brought his son, Samuel, with him to visit. While the older men talked, Samuel, a headstrong impetuous youth, chatted happily with Bridget in the garden.

Bridget enjoyed the young man's company and encouraged him to call again. Soon Samuel was a regular visitor. Sir Francis watched the affection develop between his mistress and the vicar's son. Their happy laughter annoyed him and he grew jealous of their private jokes.

One afternoon, when Samuel was walking home from Maesyfelin, three ruffians assailed him. He fought valiantly but was no match for the brutes. They gave the youth a beating. His body was found floating in the Teifi the following day. The vicar had no proof that Sir Francis had ordered the murder, but in his heart he knew the truth and called on God to avenge the death of his son.

When Sir Francis died, his son Charles inherited the estate but committed suicide a short time later. The second son, Lucius inherited. He was a gambler and wagered the whole estate in a bet, with his brother-in-law, on who would die first. He died shortly after and lost the bet. Maesyfelin then passed to the brother-in-law living at nearby Peterwell House. And so, Sir Herbert Lloyd became lord and master of two estates.

Sir Herbert was a braggart and a bully who inflicted hardships on his tenants and never paid his debts. As Lord of Lampeter, he controlled the courts and had himself appointed as the Member of Parliament. He had no interest in Maesyfelin and dismantled the house, taking the stone to improve his own home. Money from the Maesyfelin Estate was plundered and squandered. A great roof garden was added to Peterwell.

Looking out from his roof garden, Sir Herbert saw a small patch of land that he did not own. He sent his henchman, Oakley, to buy the land but the peasant would not sell. When Oakley returned with the news, Sir Herbert flew into a rage. He wanted the land and no peasant was going to stand in his way. They hatched a plan.

The following day Sir Herbert's prize black ram went missing and the constable was told to investigate the theft of the animal. Two nights later Oakley and some accomplices lowered the black ram down the peasant's chimney while Sir Herbert summoned the Constable.

'Come quickly. I know who the thief is!' cried Sir Herbert.

He led the Constable to the peasant's house and banged on the door.

The peasant and his wife had just been woken by the black

ram and were confused when Sir Herbert barged his way in.

'There is your evidence,' he said, pointing at the ram.

The peasant was led away in chains. He protested his innocence at the trial, but the jury, picked by Sir Herbert, quickly found him guilty of rustling and sentence was passed: death by hanging. Later, after the sentence had been carried out, Sir Herbert produced a bill of sale as evidence that he had bought the land.

Sir Herbert tried a similar trick with another neighbour when he claimed a valuable tapestry was stolen from his house. Once more Oakley and some servants lowered the item down the victim's chimney but the plan went wrong when the tapestry caught fire. As planned, Sir Herbert burst into the house, expecting to recover his property – but the evidence had gone up in smoke.

Sir Herbert and his henchman Oakley were dangerous men. One biographer of Sir Herbert wrote:

He was regarded by his contemporaries
and later generations as the very epitome of evil.

Chronicler Elisabeth Inglis-Jones wrote about Oakley:

infamous agent, whose bastards overran the town,
who had his own methods of extorting votes for his master.

Reports show that Oakley had fourteen illegitimate children.

Pressure mounted to bring Sir Herbert down and his evil ways began to catch up with him. MPs could not be pursued for debt but, following pressure from local squires, he lost his Parliamentary seat in 1768. His creditors were, at last, able to pursue Sir Herbert for their money but he had squandered the fortunes of two great families. There was nothing left.

Within a year, Sir Herbert Lloyd killed himself. He left no heir and, because his death was a suicide, his body was buried in the dead of night. Two great houses, built using the same stone, had been destroyed. The vicar's curse had come true.

# Lampeter Walk

This is a walk that starts by climbing west up an easy gradient away from the town giving you good views of the rolling countryside and the Teifi valley with the meandering river. It then turns south and descends across farmland into the valley and returns towards Lampeter following the bank of the river. The town of Lampeter (*Llanbedr Pont Steffan*) was built at a strategic location on the Afon Teifi. Welsh is a very descriptive language and the Welsh name, 'Church of St Peter, Stephen's Bridge', tells us the names of the parish church and the crossing point on the river. Lampeter has an ancient heritage as a market town whose fairs and markets were known for their drinking and violence. Stocks and a whipping post stood outside the town hall and were in regular use during the eighteenth century.

Lampeter is 12.5 miles south-east of Aberaeron along the A482 and 21 miles north-east of Carmarthen (*Caerfyrddin*) along the A485. The walk starts west of the town centre, just past a petrol filling station, on the junction of the A475 and Maestir Road, where there is room to park.

*Ordnance Survey map number 146 grid reference SN 571 482*
Latitude = 52.1134, Longitude = -4.0884
Lat = 52 degrees, 6.8 minutes North
Long = 4 degrees, 5.3 minutes West

| | |
|---|---|
| Length | 8.77 km – 5.45 miles |
| Maximum height | 218.75m |
| Minimum height | 104.71m |
| Height ascended | 143.57m |
| Navigation | Easy |
| Difficulty | Moderate |
| Estimated time | 3 hours 12 minutes |

Leave your car and walk west along Maestir Road passing Peterwell House bed and breakfast on your left. The original Peterwell House, where Sir Herbert lived, was on the other side of the main road and the ruin is in a clump of trees. The house was demolished in 1859, although parts of the original towers remain. The site of the earlier house, Maesyfelin, which, according to the legend, was plundered by Sir Herbert, is now covered with a modern housing estate and no trace remains of it.

After 1.4 km the road levels out. Look north-east and in the distance, 4.3 km, away you will see a strange tower. This is a folly named Twr y Deri. It was built in 1837 on the orders of a local squire to provide work for unemployed men in the parish of Betws Bledrws. The tower is a listed building by the Royal Commission on the Ancient and Historical Monuments of Wales. Continue walking along Maestir Road for a further 200 m until you reach a junction, where you turn left along a lane with a blue cycle route sign.

The lane takes you west passing a spectacular line of mature birch trees on your right. After 500 m you pass on your right a farmhouse, Tŷ Llwyd. 100 m further on you leave the lane and turn left into a gated track with a footpath sign. The track goes south-east for 120m and then turns right so that you are walking south-west.

Follow the track for another 100 m until you reach a stile on the right-hand side of the track. Go over the stile into the field and walk south-west, keeping to the left-hand side of the field and next to a gorse hedge. From here the walk begins to descend and there are good views of the surrounding countryside. After 160 m, go through a gate leading to the next field and continue straight on through another gate and down the field until you reach a series of four gates, leading to a tree-lined track.

The track continues south for 400 m and brings you to a farm.

*The footpath follows the banks of the Teifi
as it meanders through the valley*

Go through the gate leading into the farmyard and then turn left, leaving the farmyard through a gate leading to a track going uphill and east. After a short distance the track turns right and takes you south for 450 m, down to the A475.

Turn left and walk along the main road for 400m until you arrive at a lane on the right signposted to 'Dolaugwyrddon Uchaf-ac-Isaf'. Turn right and walk south-east down the lane for 200 m where the lane turns south and, after another 500 m, you pass a large house on your right. Immediately after the house the lane turns left, and you leave the tarmac lane and continue straight on along a short track leading down to a stream with a ford and a narrow bridge. Cross the stream and go through the gate leading into the next field.

Walk towards the large blue slurry tank and, just before you

*A tower is all that remains of Peterwell House,*
*and it is difficult to see through the trees*

reach it, turn right so that you walk south-west and join a track following the left-hand side of the field. Continue in this direction for 240 m until you reach a stile and gate on your left. Go over the stile and walk south 60 m to the riverbank, where you turn left.

From here you walk through the fields for 2.5 km following the Teifi back towards Lampeter. Was it somewhere here that the vicar's unfortunate son was murdered and thrown into the river?

When you arrive at a solid-looking wooden bridge with a gate at each end, stop and turn left immediately before the bridge so that you are walking north, away from the river, with a stream on your right. After 220 m you go through a metal gate leading to a track that continues north along the right hand side of the next field.

At the next gate, 250 m further on, look across the field on your left. There is a clump of trees and all that remains of Peterwell, the great house, with its magnificent roof garden, where Sir Herbert spied on his neighbours and planned his evil deeds. Continue north along the track until you see the footpath leaving to the right. Walk across the next small field towards wooden steps leading over a stone wall and back to the road junction where the walk began.

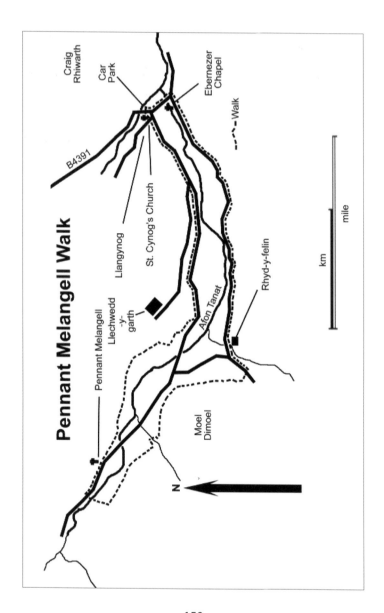

# Pennant Melangell Walk

Craig Rhiwarth

Car Park

Ebernezer Chapel

- - - Walk

B4391

Llangynog

St. Cynog's Church

Pennant Melangell

Llechwedd -y- garth

Afon Tanat

Rhyd-y-felin

Moel Dimoel

N

km

mile

## 15

# Melangell and the Hare

Melangell was an Irish princess, born in the seventh century. As a girl she had great beauty and charm. Melangell grew into an intelligent and serene young woman with a calmness that all admired. Her father, the king, chose a noble of high birth for Melangell to marry. When he told the princess she was to be wed, she refused to accept her suitor. The king persisted. He cajoled and bullied. He ranted and threatened but it made no difference. Melangell did not argue with her father, that was not her way, but her stubbornness made him realise she would never marry the nobleman.

Furious with his daughter for being so selfish, the king banished her from his kingdom forever. The young princess left Ireland and sailed away, never to return. She crossed the sea and landed in the kingdom of Powys where she made her way across the mountains to the hidden valley of Pennant, a place so remote and wild that no one would ever find her.

Melangell found a crevice in the rock face with a stone slab on the floor. She fetched bracken to make a bed and the tiny cave became her home. Melangell passed the days wandering the Berwyn Mountains collecting berries, seeds and honey. Her diet was meagre. She gathered wool caught in the hawthorn bushes and wove simple garments to replace her tattered rags.

Her life was hard but Melangell was not alone; she had God as her daily companion. Each morning, before she went foraging,

Melangell would pray. She chatted gaily to God like an old friend. Each night before she lay down on her stone slab to rest, she would go down on her knees and beg forgiveness for her sins that day.

This was Melangell's life for fifteen years. She lived alone and forgotten by the world, for no man of woman ever ventured into her hidden valley. One bright spring morning, while Melangell was saying her prayers, she heard the sound of hunting horns echoing along the valley. There was a haunting baying of hunting dogs and the thunder of horse's hooves.

A hare darted across the ground and under Melangell's cloak. The princess remained on her knees and calmly continued to pray, as the huntsmen appeared. The dogs gathered around the kneeling woman but would not approach. They could see the hare hiding beneath Melangell's cloak, and in their lust for blood they snapped and snarled at her.

A huntsman lifted his horn to his lips and blew but there was no sound. Melangell went on praying and, slowly, the hounds grew quiet. They sat and waited. The horses stopped prancing and stood still with steam rising from their flanks. The men watched in silence as Melangell finished her devotions, stood up and walked towards them. The hare hopped along beneath her coat. As the woman got closer the dogs and the horses began to back away.

'Who are you? What are you doing on my land?' demanded one of the riders.

'I am Melangell and this is my home,' replied the princess calmly.

The rider, who had spoken, dismounted and took off his gloves. He surveyed the woman. Her clothes were shabby but he saw she was no peasant.

'I am Brochwel, prince of Powys,' he said. 'You have cowed my horses and silenced my hounds. You are brave, Melangell,' added Brochwel.

'It is not bravery to let a frightened animal shelter under my skirts, my lord. Your dogs are fierce and your men outnumber the hare,' said Melangell.

The prince of Powys considered her answer for a moment and then he laughed. 'You are right, Melangell. My dogs are fierce and we are many, so I say this. The hare can stay here with you and I give you this valley as a sanctuary for the frightened and the weak.'

The prince remounted and turned his steed.

'Gentlemen, let us find bigger prey to hunt this day,' he cried and spurred his horse forward down the valley. Melangell watched as the hunters disappeared from view, while the hare sat quietly nibbling at the grass, by the feet of its protector.

As news of Melangell's courage and the prince's gift of the valley spread, pious women, wanting to live a good life, joined Melangell. They built a chapel in God's honour and, as the prince had said, tended to the frightened and the weak that arrived seeking help. Melangell lived as the abbess of her holy community for another thirty-five years. When she died her bones were interred in a shrine within the church.

1300 years after her death, Princess Melangell is still venerated, and Pennant Melangell remains a quiet place of retreat for the sick and frightened of this world.

# Cwm Pennant Walk

We did this walk on a bright sunny day in March. Cwm Pennant is a delightful valley and signs of spring were everywhere. Crocuses peeped from the hedgerows, blowsy daffodils waved in the sunshine, and the fields were alive with lambs, busy exploring the strange world they had just entered. The church at Pennant Melangell is unusual. It is a pilgrimage church and has no regular congregation. Each day at noon, the priest reads prayers left by the pilgrims. It is a spiritual place, and a very enjoyable valley to walk in.

Part of the route is in woodland that is used for rearing game birds, where the footpaths pass through fenced areas. To deter predators, the 2-metre-high fences are electrified with bare wires. If they are switched on it is possible to get a nasty shock, so take care, particularly if there are children in your party. The walk starts in the village of Llangynog, located on the B4391 ten miles south-east of Bala. There are public toilets and a free car park on Berwyn Street.

*Ordnance Survey map number 124 grid reference SJ 053 260*
Latitude = 52.8246, Longitude = -3.4060
Lat = 52 degrees, 49.5 minutes North
Long = 3 degrees, 24.4 minutes West

| | |
|---|---|
| Length | 8.74 km – 5.43 miles |
| Maximum height | 286.49 m |
| Minimum height | 158.35 m |
| Height ascended | 316.64 m |
| Navigation | Easy |
| Difficulty | Moderate |
| Estimated time | 3 hours 45 minutes |

*The lane climbs gently into Cwm Pennant*

Walk south along Berwyn Street and turn right along the lane immediately after St Cynog's church. Walk west along the lane for 660 m as it climbs gently away from the village. Bear left at the fork in the road and descend towards the river. The right-hand fork leads to Llechweddygarth, where the guns meet before a day's sport. The river on your left is the Tanat, which flows east into Shropshire before returning to Wales and joining the Afon Efyrnwy. Continue along the lane for another 1.18 km until you reach a driveway on your right leading to Vicarage Farm.

Immediately after the driveway, follow the footpath sign and turn right, through a gate leading into a field. Walk north-west across the field for 150 m and through two more gates, where you continue straight on following the yellow footpath signs and the left-hand side of the field. Turn right at the corner of the field and walk north following the path as it climbs to the top of the field.

When you reach the top turn left through the gap and walk north-west aiming for a gate, leading to a track, on the far side of the field. Turn right and walk 50 m along the track to the next gate where you keep following the track as it climbs and starts to turn to the left. After 200 m there is another gate across the track where you continue straight on. Another 100 m will bring you to a house and outbuildings. Walk across the gravel parking area below the outbuildings and downhill along the grassy track opposite so that you are walking north-west.

The mountain on your left is Moel Dimoel and, according to another legend, is where the giant Cawr Berwyn leapt from the top of the mountain and landed in the farmyard at the bottom of the valley called Rhyd-y-felin. If you look directly south you will see the farm in the valley.

Continue along the track, through a wooden gate and go straight on, following the line of trees until the path descends towards the river. Once you reach the valley floor continue west, with a wire fence on your left, and aim for the church further along the valley. After 200 m you go through a gate and continue straight on until the footpath joins a track heading towards the church. Go through the gate leading to the parking area and through the lych gate into the churchyard.

The church is normally open. Inside the steeple, reached through a wooden door inside the church, there is an interesting exhibition describing the history of the valley and its people. There is a large whalebone, mounted in the nave wall which, it is claimed, is the saint's rib and was found in Melangell's grave. Another explanation is that it was the rib bone of the giant mentioned earlier.

Leave the church through the parking area and turn right along the lane for 350 m until you reach a footpath sign and stile, leading down to a footbridge on your left. Cross the stile, the

*Pennant Melangell church*

footbridge over the river and a second stile leading into a field. From here you walk south across the field and up a steep bank aiming for a wooden signpost just in front of the tree-line. This is a deviation from the footpath shown on the Ordnance Survey maps but is clearly marked on the ground.

There is a stile leading into a wood just beyond the signpost, which you cross, and turn left along a path that follows the bottom edge of the wood. The woods are part of Llechweddygarth Estate, which covers 5000 acres. The birds are reared intensively and then, when the time comes, driven by beaters towards the guns. You will hear pheasants calling as you walk and may be startled by birds that you have disturbed, suddenly taking off close by. The bird enclosures in the woods do get moved about but the paths are not difficult to follow so, to avoid confusion, I have not recorded the fences and gates.

Follow the path south-east for 300 m through the wood until you arrive at the bottom of the hill and a gate leading to a field on your left. When we did this walk, there was a toy London bus tied to the top of the left-hand gatepost, possibly a 'Geocache' left by someone engaging in the new hobby, spawned by GPS technology. It may be still there.

Do not go through the gate. Instead, continue straight on along the path with the stone wall on your left. This will bring you to a house. The footpath goes behind the house. Keep close to the fence on your left and go through the small wooden gate on the far corner behind the house. The path goes along the back of the barn and emerges through two more gates, where it continues south-west following a stream across a field and back towards the forest. Cross the stream and go over the stile leading into the trees, where you turn left following the path south through the wood for 500 m until you arrive at a stile. The path is indistinct in places but generally keeps near to the fence line.

Turn left over the stile and walk downhill keeping to the right-hand side of the field. There is a stile at the bottom of the field leading to a lane. Go over the stile and turn left along the lane. After 170 m you pass Rhyd-y-felin, the farm where, legend says, the giant landed after his mighty leap.

From here you have a pleasant walk for 2.2 km down a quiet country lane along the bottom of the valley with the river on your left.

As you approach Llangynog look at the mountain to your north-east, beyond the village. This is Craig Rhiwarth, and on its peak sat one of the highest hill forts in Wales. It is believed that the fort contained over 170 circular buildings, some of which were over 12 m in diameter. The fort was probably abandoned about the time of the Roman invasion.

The caves that you can see below the summit were part of

*Craig Rhiwarth: the caves are in the centre of the picture,
and the incline is to the left*

slate workings on the mountain. The slate was quarried before being moved around the mountain on lateral tramways and slid down to the valley on an incline, which can be seen just to the left of the cave entrances. Once down the mountain the slate was split and machined using water-power. Lead and granite were also mined on the mountain and at one time Llangynog was the largest lead-mining area in Europe. At the time, over 2000 men worked in the industry and there were seven pubs in the village. Today, the population is less than 200. Look again at the caves. According to local talk, an old woman has taken up residence in the caves and can often been seen, outside the entrance, washing her clothes in a giant copper pan.

When you reach the T-junction at the end of the lane turn left at the Ebenezer Chapel and walk over the bridge. From here, you follow the road across the valley and back to the car park.

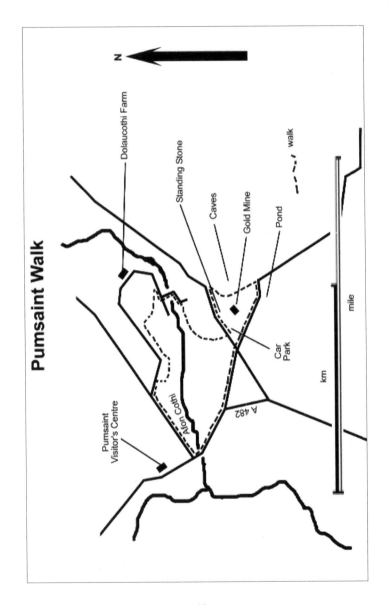

Pumsaint Walk

Dolaucothi Farm

Standing Stone

Caves

Gold Mine

Pond

walk

Car Park

A 482

Afon Cothi

Pumsaint Visitor's Centre

km

mile

N

# 16

# The Five Saints

Cynyr ap Cunedda and his wife lived in the sixth century, in the little village of Caio. When his wife told him she was expecting a child Cynyr's heart filled with pride and love for his wife. The day of her confinement arrived and the women of the village gathered to help deliver the baby. But there was not just one child delivered that night; there were five and they were all sons. It was a miracle and the people rejoiced when they heard the news.

The boys were named Ceitho, Gwyn, Gwynno, Gwynnoro and Celynin. Cynyr gave thanks to God for his good fortune and vowed to raise them as devout Christians.

'They will live the lives of saints,' promised the proud Father.

There was no school in the village but, as the boys grew, their priest taught them letters and to write their names.

One day, a tinker came to the village with news. St David was coming to preach at Llanddewi Brefi. The priest went to the boy's Father.

'Cynyr, you must send your sons to hear the great man speak,' said the priest.

It was agreed and the next day the five young men left Caio to travel north and hear St David's sermon.

Not far from Caio, the road passes the caves of Ogufau, a dank and forbidding place. An evil, jealous wizard lived in the caves. He heard the five brothers chatting happily as they approached. The wizard summoned great storm clouds. A fierce wind howled between the mountains. Darkness smothered the land and rain began to fall in torrents. Thunder boomed across the valley and lightning bolted across the heavens.

The five brothers grew weary as they tried to continue their journey but the rain and the wind were too strong.

'We cannot go on,' cried Ceitho.

'We must stop,' yelled Gwyn.

A great weariness had come over the brothers, brought on by the sorcerer's spell.

'Let us rest by that rock,' called Celynin.

The five brothers sat down with their backs resting against a giant boulder. They tried to stay awake but the sorcerer's spell was too powerful. Soon all five were asleep. The rain turned to hail that was so violent it pushed the boys faces deep into the stone. The wicked wizard had trapped the brothers. The wizard emerged from his cave and released the sleeping boys from the rock that was holding them. Then, he dragged them into the caves of Ogufau and down into the bowels of the earth.

After the five brothers vanished, a young woman named Gweno, who was their friend, went looking for them. She went into the caves and slowly made her way through the subterranean passages, passing deeper and deeper into the ground, until she reached a strange chamber. In the middle of the chamber stood a pillar. There was a small opening on the far side of the chamber. Gweno went towards it.

Suddenly, freezing water flooded into the chamber. The force of the water swept her off her feet. She struggled to stand but the water level rose until her head pressed against the roof of the cave. Gweno gulped for air. Something hard and cold gripped her ankles. She kicked out, trying to break free but the hold was too strong. Slowly her tired body was pulled beneath the surface. With one last piercing scream she vanished, down into the depths of the underworld. The people call the cavern where Gweno vanished 'Clochdy Gweno' (*clochdy* = belfry). It lies deep in the ground but the ghost of Gweno still roams the Ogufau caves. Her spirit vapour sometimes appears as a white mist while she moans and wails to be released from her fetid subterranean grave, in the rocks below.

The five brothers were never seen again. They are still slumbering somewhere in the caves, ready to wake when King Arthur returns or, according to Bishop Baldwin's writing in 1188, when a truly apostolic prelate occupies the throne of St David.

Fifteen centuries later, the giant boulder where the brothers slept is still there. Look closely. Can you see where their faces were pushed into the rock on that dreadful day?

# Pumsaint Walk

This is one of the shorter walks in this series with very little climbing except a short stretch above the Dolaucothi Gold Mine. The walk takes you through part of the Dolaucothi Estate which is now owned by the National Trust, includes a stroll along the bank of Afon Cothi and takes you along an old drovers track above the gold mine, past caves and entrances to old mine workings. Pumsaint (*pump* = five) is located on the A482, 8 miles north west of Llandovery (*Llanymddyfri*). Follow the signposts for the gold mine where there is a car park, toilets for visitors and a picnic area. It is possible to join National Trust guided tours of the mine and pan for gold but you should check the opening times beforehand since the mine is closed to the public on certain days of the week and out of season. There is also a visitor centre and public toilets in Pumsaint, which would involve a small detour from the walk.

***Ordnance Survey map number 146 grid reference SN 6621 403***
Latitude = 52.0451, Longitude = -3.9517
Lat = 52 degrees, 2.7 minutes North
Long = 3 degrees, 57.1 minutes West

| | |
|---|---|
| Length | 3.22 Km – 2 miles. |
| Maximum height | 183.63m |
| Minimum height | 122.63m |
| Height ascended | 104.13m |
| Navigation | Easy |
| Difficulty | Easy |
| Estimated time | 1 hour 30 minutes |

Leave your car and walk north east along the lane. After 100m you reach a grassy clearing on your right where you will see a large standing stone on a mound of earth. This is the stone that, according to legend, the five saints reclined against and fell asleep. The indentations caused by their faces can be seen on the sides of the rock. I have looked closely and can only find four. See if you can do better and find the fifth face.

The Ogofau Mine was a major producer of gold during the Roman occupation and there was an important fort named Luentinum located at Pumsaint. Serious mining started in AD75 when thousands of slaves were employed in the mine and gold was shipped from Dolaucothi to an imperial mint in

*The rock the five saints rested against*

Lyon, France. The Romans built a number of dams and aqueducts to harness waterpower for the mine. The longest watercourse they built for the mine was seven miles long. The rock you have been looking at was an anvil used in a Roman water powered crushing mill to crush the ore as it was brought out from the mine. This was the first step in extracting the gold. As it wore, the anvil was rotated to use the other sides, causing the indentations in the rock.

Although gold has not been mined at Dolaucothi since 1938, it is still highly valued and Welsh gold is used for royal wedding rings.

Continue along the lane for 150m until you reach a track and leave the lane at a sharp right hand turn, just before a green forestry sign. There is no footpath sign but you turn right and follow the path. This is an old drover's track from Caio, used over the centuries to move livestock to avoid paying toll charges. As you follow the track you will see how the rocks have worn over the years with the passing of thousands of animals. This is the route the saints would have used as they passed the Ogofau caves. The path climbs south west for a short distance and then turns south. Below you, on your right, you will see the mine and, as you reach the top of the climb, you will find a large cave on your left. The mountain is riddled with old workings and this is an entrance to an upper level of the mine. On the other hand, it may have been the wizard's home!

Continue on past the cave until you reach a tarmac road where you turn right and walk downhill. After a short distance you pass a man made pond on your left, part of the old water system. This pond was drained in the last century revealing Roman pottery and other artefacts. The mine continued sporadic gold production until 1938 when it was closed. Extensive research and archaeological work has been done on the mine and the surrounding area and some spectacular gold objects unearthed, including a gold chain over 1 metre long and weighing a staggering 1.2kg. The gold items that were recovered have been dated to the second or third century AD and are now held at the British Museum as part of the Payne Knight Collection.

After 320m, you reach a crossroads where you go straight across, following the lane downhill for a further 300m until you reach the main road. Turn right at the main road and walk towards Pumsaint. Cross the Cothi and turn right along a track just after the river bridge. If you want to see the visitor's centre, continue on along the road for another 150m where you will find it on your right. To rejoin the walk, retrace your steps back to the start of the track.

Follow the track north east for 650m until you arrive at a right turn signposted to 'Dolaucothi Farm B & B'. Turn right and follow the track towards the farm for 120m until it turns to the left. Leave the track at the corner and continue straight on along a path

*The drovers' track from Caio*

signposted by a National Trust footpath sign, a white arrow on a red circle. After 30m turn right through a gap in the hedge at the side of the path, shown by a similar sign, and go down some steps to a stile.

Before you cross the stile, turn and look to your left where you will find an unusual spring covered by a stone arch and a tree, which has grown right over the top of the arch. Having crossed the stile, walk along the left hand side of the field to the next stile. As you walk towards the stile there is a 'ha-ha' on your left, built to give uninterrupted views from the house while keeping animals out of the garden. On your right there are mature trees dotted across the field, suggesting this was parkland and part of a high status property at one time. The Dolaucothi Estate was owned by a number of wealthy families including the Earl of Cawdor. Two

*The cave the saints passed on their fateful journey*

other notable owners were John and Henry Harries, wizards and conjurers, famous throughout south Wales in the nineteenth century.

Traverse the next stile and follow the footpath along the side of a high stone wall on your left. Where the wall ends, continue straight on over a stile and through a gate to the Afon Cothi. Turn right and follow the bank of the river for a short distance until you reach a stone bridge. Cross the river, using the bridge, and walk along the track passing a picnic area on your right, next to the river. After 60m turn right over a stile and take the path along the south bank of the river. The path follows the river for a short distance and then bears left, bringing you back to the entrance of the gold mine and the end of your walk.